WALKING IN THE PEAK DISTRICT – WHITE PEAK WEST

40 WALKS IN THE HILLS OF CHESHIRE, DERBYSHIRE AND STAFFORDSHIRE

About the Author

Paul Besley has spent a lifetime walking through the dales and villages of the White Peak. His interest is in the human interaction with landscape. His love of the ancient – whether it is a Neolithic burial chamber, a Norman church or the medieval ridge and furrow landscape – has provided him with thousands of hours of enjoyment. His desire to pass on his experiences has always informed his writing.

He is a regular contributor to magazines. His writing has taken him across Britain and across the world, working on varied subject matter. He is a team member of Mountain Rescue and a dog handler in Mountain Rescue Search Dogs England with his Border collie. He lives in Sheffield with his wife, metalsmith Alison Counsell and their three dogs Olly, Monty and search dog Scout.

WALKING IN THE PEAK DISTRICT – WHITE PEAK WEST

40 WALKS IN THE HILLS OF CHESHIRE, DERBYSHIRE AND STAFFORDSHIRE

by Paul Besley

JUNIPER HOUSE, MURLEY MOSS,
OXENHOLME ROAD, KENDAL, CUMBRIA LA9 7RL
www.cicerone.co.uk

© Paul Besley 2021
First edition 2021
ISBN: 978 1 85284 977 1

Printed in Singapore by KHL Printing on responsibly sourced paper
All photographs are by the author unless otherwise stated.
A catalogue record for this book is available from the British Library.

© Crown copyright 2021 OS PU100012932

This book is dedicated to the members of Coniston Mountain Rescue, without whose aid it would not have been possible. Thank you.

Updates to this guide

While every effort is made by our authors to ensure the accuracy of guide-books as they go to print, changes can occur during the lifetime of an edition. This guidebook was researched before and finalised during the COVID-19 pandemic. While we are not aware of any significant changes to routes or facilities at the time of printing, it is likely that the current situation will give rise to more changes than would usually be expected. Any updates that we know of for this guide will be on the Cicerone website (www.cicerone.co.uk/977/updates), so please check before planning your trip. We also advise that you check information about such things as transport, accommodation and shops locally. Even rights of way can be altered over time.

We are always grateful for information about any discrepancies between a guidebook and the facts on the ground, sent by email to updates@cicerone.co.uk or by post to Cicerone, Juniper House, Murley Moss, Oxenholme Road, Kendal, LA9 7RL.

Register your book: To sign up to receive free updates, special offers and GPX files where available, register your book at www.cicerone.co.uk.

Front cover: Three Shires Head, where the three counties of Cheshire, Derbyshire and Staffordshire meet (Walk 16)

CONTENTS

Acknowledgements

I got to enjoy many days out while researching this final volume of the Peak District trilogy. The beautiful scenery is perhaps a given, but what always adds to a day is the interaction with other people – walkers, climbers, cavers, local people and those working on the land. Everyone helped in some way to contribute to the overall message of the book. Our countryside is not just about the land, but perhaps more importantly, it is about the people. To all of you, I want to say thank you for making my days that much richer.

I owe a big thank you to the team at Cicerone Press, Joe Williams, Amy Hodkin, Andrea Grimshaw, Clare Crooke, Caroline Draper, Hannah Stevenson and Felicity Laughton.

Some people gave more than a few words and accompanied me on the walks, checked the accuracy of the directions and generally kept nudging me forward. I would like to specifically thank Alison Counsell, Gail and John Ferriman. And a special mention to Scout, my Border collie walking companion.

Thank you to Ian Bunting of the Peak District Mountain Rescue Organisation for his help in the history of PDMRO. To Mel Bale and David Morton of the Peak and Northern Footpaths Society for all their help and advice, once again, and to that society as a whole for providing such beautiful signposts that for many years have instilled a feeling of confidence in many walkers by giving onward directions. To Nic Bunting of the Hathersage shop, Outside, who manages to sell more of these Peak District books than anyone else I know. You paid for a few chippy teas for me, and sausages for Scout at the end of a walking day. Sarah Simpson and her apple orchards. Finally, Robert Adam of Townend Farm for allowing me to watch the sheep shearing.

A walk isn't a walk without a dog, and I would like to thank Monty, Olly and Scout for their contribution, and for never sharing their food but always sharing mine.

Most important of all Alison Counsell, my partner of many years. You made all the difference.

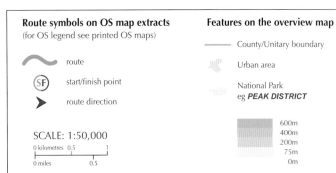

Route symbols on OS map extracts
(for OS legend see printed OS maps)

~ route

(SF) start/finish point

➤ route direction

SCALE: 1:50,000

0 kilometres 0.5   1

0 miles   0.5

Features on the overview map

—————— County/Unitary boundary

Urban area

National Park
eg **PEAK DISTRICT**

600m
400m
200m
75m
0m

GPX files for all routes can be downloaded free at www.cicerone.co.uk/977/GPX.

Combs Moss from Corbar Hill (Walk 9)

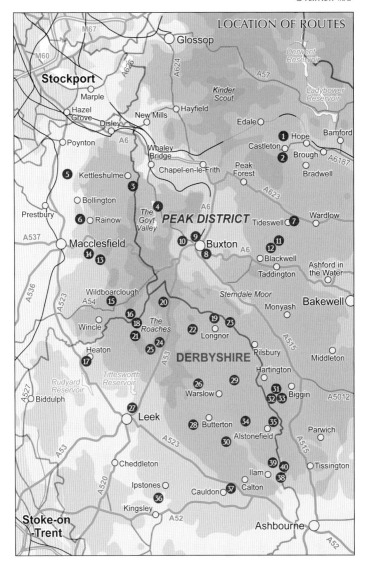

LOCATION OF ROUTES

Scout with the Revidge Dragon and, in the distance, the Dragon's Back (Walk 29)

INTRODUCTION

Combs Moss trig and the high moors of the Dark Peak beyond (Walk 9)

Within the Peak District we are fortunate to have a landscape that comprises three different environments, three different days out, three different experiences. The northern Dark Peak, rugged, windswept, full of big skies and tumultuous days; the eastern White Peak, ancient, historical, pastoral, full of pretty villages with beautiful churches and gentle rolling hills; and the western White Peak, the ramparts of the Dark Peak gritstone holding down the limestone centre, full of pasture and moorland, towns, villages and people.

There is something town and country about the landscape covered in this third and final book of the Peak District trilogy. Perhaps it is its proximity to, and spread into, the towns, once centres of industry, now often dormitories for the cities of the west and Midlands. The landscape is more human, actively human, there are more farms here, or seem to be, than anywhere else in the Peak District. And there is that odd collision of high moorland with their grouse shoots and pocket-sized spaces of ruggedness, looking down on the ancient farms, the drove roads and the salt routes that nod to and follow the old roads the Romans made across the hills and dales. And those dales that run from watershed to the seas, east and west, are cut with the meandering crystal-clear waters of the Dove, Hamps, Manifold, Dane and Goyt, home to trout, crayfish, dipper and vole, their banks lined with wild garlic and old oak. The whole is buttressed by the country towns of Leek, Macclesfield and Buxton, while in the west the industrial homeland of Manchester constantly shimmers in the distance. Beyond lies the great Cheshire Plain and beyond that the Welsh mountains stand like a shadow on the horizon.

The western White Peak area for this book begins in the north. Gritstone stands erect on the hills, holding back the peat moorlands. This is climbing country, the long stretches of Kinder Grit and Millstone providing routes and tests that could last a person a lifetime. Windgather Rocks sits so close to the road that you could almost step out of the car and straight onto rock. Seeing all those brightly coloured human flies working their way up the walls makes for a great spectacle. Of course, The Roaches, that line of gritstone with the ski jump of Hen Cloud at the end, is the jewel in the crown; some say it's the most iconic of gritstone edges in the Dark Peak after Stanage. The gritstone line finishes at Ramshaw Rocks, which winks at you as you travel down the Roman road that we now call the A53.

This land tells a story of travel in the roads of silk and salt and beast that radiated out from Cheshire. Yes, the silk roads are not just some Eastern legend. The Peak silk routes wound their way from the villages, hamlets and farmsteads of the western Peak, crossing valleys and rivers over beautiful stone packhorse bridges, some now long forgotten and a delight to discover. Ending in Upper Hulme or Macclesfield, the silk brought wealth for a time, apparent in the growth of the communities and development of fine buildings. The salt roads that spread out like the fingers of a hand from the mines of Cheshire brought great fortune to the Cheshire lords, and means of food preservation to the growing population. Along the drove roads, huge herds of sheep and cattle were transported over the moors. The cattle were shod for the long journey. The road at Herbage, once an important stopping place, is still clearly visible (Walk 26).

Inside the gritstone girdle sits the limestone bed, and this can be seen most clearly around Buxton and Castleton. Castleton has Winnats Pass, the awesome limestone gorge that holds the caves that made the village rich and famous. And no walker can ignore Buxton, with its huge limestone quarries nibbling off chunks of the landscape to satisfy our need for roads, homes and paved gardens.

Moving further south, the area becomes more Norman, more monastic, encroaching as it does

An ancient trade route approaching Saltersford Hall. The name tells us that this was once a salt route for packhorses (Walk 6)

onto the medieval landscapes of the eastern side of the White Peak. Here are the limestone reefs of Chrome Hill and Parkhouse, great gnarled hunchbacks of rock that seem to have been picked up by a giant and placed delicately between secluded dales. The settlements that prospered in the 14th and 15th centuries, when sheep were the main industry, are now beautiful villages with hidden lanes and alleys to explore. The surrounding land, drawn and divided by limestone walls, allows us to see the development of the haves and have nots: starting with long, narrow fields close to the village, the enclosures get ever larger as each iteration took more land away from commoners, until nought was left that wasn't held by those with money.

In the centre are the dales. Beautiful rivers that wind their way through the landscape create a meandering pattern of water meadows, pasture and ancient hedgerows that line the old ways across the dales. The limestone here towers in huge spikes, in clumps that look like some great natural cathedral organ waiting to be brought to life. The caves are vast and a delight to explore for children of all ages. And as you follow the water downstream you'll come upon a landscape that has been frozen in time. Norman churches abound and there are country estates with grand houses. Large communities, once busy with weaving, cheese making or quarrying, now act as centres of recreation, providing a start and end to many walks and a place to obtain food and accommodation.

The walks are not particularly long or onerous. This is a landscape to be enjoyed slowly; the more time spent the more there is to enjoy. Rest regularly against an old oak or a limestone wall and look around you. Imagine what it would be like to walk the silk route. Time is the most precious thing we have; we can use it wisely here.

THE LANDSCAPE

The landscape is a product of time. What we walk over is a creation, both natural and human. The plateau of limestone has been cut by water, producing deep dales and steep grassy slopes. Weather too has played a huge part in influencing the landscape. The limestone formed 350 million years ago. Skeletal remains of sea creatures gradually descended to a tropical seabed and, over time, layer upon layer formed the limestone we see today. At points, the limestone bed is at least 1.2 miles (2km) thick, and can hold deposits of galena, fluorspar and copper, among others, the results of volcanic activity we would not normally associate with this area. On the fringes stand the ramparts of the Pennine range, the Namurian Millstone Grit, forming the last visible outcrops of the vast river delta that carried the sediments down from central Europe and lay them across the limestone bed. The acidic soil on the limestone provides an environment for good pasture and grazing, while the peaty coarse soils provide a suitable habitat for the heath and moorland that is typical of the gritstone upland.

Glacial melt waters formed the dales, the characteristic U-shaped valleys that run throughout the limestone plateau. Some valleys, such as Hay Dale, were formed by the glacial waters scouring out the landscape as they moved towards the great rivers. Others, for instance Dovedale, were formed by water cutting out the limestone rock, leaving the huge caves and towers that dot the limestone crags – a testament to the power of water as it cut its way through the remains of the billions of sea creatures that formed the limestone. The process continues today, as the crystal-clear rivers amble down the dales, removing more of the physical presence of the seabed.

Farming has been a major activity in the White Peak for many centuries.

Ilam Rock is a classic limestone pinnacle (Walk 38)

A water vole on the banks of the River Dove (Walk 38)

The number of 'granges' tell of the extent of monastic holding during the Middle Ages, when the region was a world centre for the production of wool. Today sheep can still be seen on the upland pastures and the slopes of the dales, including the hardy black and white-faced Derbyshire Gritstone sheep, bred for these parts. As farming developed, the need for water, always a problem in an upland porous limestone landscape, needed to be solved, and man-made dewponds were used to gather and store water. Many have fallen into disuse, but there are some that still provide the water needed for livestock and wildlife.

PLANTS AND WILDLIFE

Many of the dales have semi-natural woodland, ancient in human terms. The trees stretch down to the rivers and streams on the dale floor. There is a mix of broadleaved species, the most prevalent being ash. In recent years ash dieback has devastated these old woodlands and many of the trees have been lost; while denuding the slopes of the dales, it has also opened up natural vistas and the sight of many limestone crags not seen for hundreds of years.

The dales are a haven for wildlife and plants. The dipper is often to be found skipping from stone to stone, while the natural crayfish thrives in the clear waters. On the riverbanks the water vole arranges its environment. Dovedale is a place where all this can often be seen, accompanied in spring and early summer by the heady aroma of wild garlic. Some dales offer a different environment. Monk's Dale, with its steeply wooded slopes forming a dark, damp environment, is a place where mosses and fungi thrive, the ancient stone walls and rotting trees covered in a carpet of numerous species.

15

HISTORY

Humans arrived in the White Peak in the Neolithic period. Dotted around the landscape, on high ground, are the remains of burial chambers and cairns, where our forebears placed their most important citizens. Five Wells chambered cairn that sits above Monsal Dale is a good example. Neolithic and Bronze Age artefacts have been discovered in many of the caves that are to be found in the dales.

The Romans arrived in the area, looking for lead and other materials to be mined. Little is left of their strongholds, but their roads, long and straight across the landscape, can still be seen. Both Batham Gate, north of Buxton, and The Street, that rises from the Goyt Valley, are good examples.

With the arrival of the Normans, land administration became more regulated. Peveril Castle, high above Castleton, was essentially an administrative outpost of William the Conqueror. The Normans, like the Romans, were interested in exploiting the lead that was in veins of the limestone.

As the population grew, settlements were established. The need for the community to feed itself meant they developed an agricultural system that suited both their needs and the landscape. At Chelmorton, you can see the strip field system surrounding the village: the thin fields are separated by rough limestone walls and bisected by wide lanes. Later, the parliamentary enclosures produced a

Peveril Castle. This Norman castle watched over the important lead-mining area (Walk 2)

more uniform field pattern and size, as common lands were taken and enclosed by private landowners for food and more predominantly for livestock. Eventually the upper pastures and moorlands were enclosed, and today little common land survives.

The Industrial Revolution brought transport to the western half of the White Peak. Many of the villages and hamlets on the fringes of Leek produced silk thread that was then transported by packhorse to the mills in Macclesfield. The route from Hollinsclough to Macclesfield Forest can still be traced today and has some beautiful packhorse bridges, such as the one near Hollinsclough (Walk 22). Salt from the Cheshire mines also crossed the area, and the routes often formed significant meeting places, such as the junction of three routes by Jenkin Chapel below Pym Chair (Walk 6). With the growth of industry, better forms of transport were required to take advantage of the economic boom that was beginning to change the face of the country.

The canal system was the first major change since the Romans built their roads. It stretches all the way down the western side of the area, connecting the southern tip with the industrial heartland of Manchester. Originally developed for the transportation of cotton and coal, the canals were a major source of economic prosperity. But the arrival of the railways soon put the canals under such pressure that they were unable to survive. However, before that happened, one of the major achievements was to connect the canals in Whaley Bridge and Cromford with a railway line that rose over 300 metres to cross the high moors, with inclines as steep as 1:7 (Walk 4).

The canals and the railways were lost for some time after motor transport became the normal way to carry goods and people around the country. Today the canals are seeing a resurgence as a place of leisure, and scenes of canalside pubs and restaurants, such as the ones at Froghall and Bollington, are now commonplace. Although the railways have gone, they have given the area a fine network of flat trails that can be enjoyed by everyone. The Cromford and High Peak railway line over the Goyt Valley, mentioned above, gives easy access to the moorlands. And of course, the Monsal Trail, the long flat line that ran from Bakewell to Buxton, is a feat of engineering, with its tunnels and viaducts providing a safe route for cyclists and walkers alike.

TWO IMPORTANT PEAK DISTRICT ORGANISATIONS

When most people think about the Peak District, the national park is generally the first organisation that comes to mind. The Peak District National Park was Britain's first national outdoor space, opening its doors, or perhaps it should be gates, in 1951. The visitor centre at Castleton offers

The Macclesfield Canal towpath provides a pleasant way back to Bollington (Walk 5)

good information about the work of the park and interesting facts about the immediate area. But before the national park there were organisations that had been working for the landscape and people.

Peak and Northern Footpaths Society
The quaintly named Peak and Northern Footpaths Society, whose roots stretch way back to the early 19th century, is perhaps the most visible to walkers. The work of this organisation is one reason we have such a good footpath network.

On almost every walk, you will come across a square, green, cast-metal sign pointing the way in white lettering. The footpath sign serves an important purpose in indicating the way of the often-inconspicuous footpath. Each sign is numbered and includes a logo of the Peak and

Northern Footpaths Society. The signs are justifiably famous, and often a welcome sight on a walk when the navigator has been in a deep discussion and has failed to keep abreast of where you actually are. The signs and the society have a long history.

From its base in Manchester, the Peak and Northern Footpath Society can trace its lineage back to 1826 and the protection of public rights of way around the Flixton area, where a landowner was trying to prevent legal access to a footpath. It has remained a strong defender of the footpath network ever since, using its extensive records and maps, and many footpath inspectors to regularly report on issues. If necessary, the society will take a case to the court to protect legal access and rights of way. The society has reported on and helped to resolve many access issues. Along with protecting access by installing signs, the society also installs bridges to aid the safe passage of people. If you come across an access issue, the details can be relayed to the society via the form on the website.

It is a charitable organisation whose costs are met by subscriptions, donations and legacies. Throughout its history, the work of the society has been closely linked to that of the outdoor movement. During that time, many reservoirs have been built, villages have been lost and footpaths have become submerged. The towns and cities surrounding the area have grown and have brought, with the increase in population, a need to get outdoors and, consequently, a constant watch on the footpath network, not just in the Peak District, but into the Midlands and areas of the North.

The society provided advice and support not just about footpaths, but

Peak and Northern Footpaths sign

also about the land. In 1922 the society noted that they would be pleased if the National Trust were to acquire the 'beautiful mountain gorge' of Dovedale. Today Dovedale is one of the most popular areas within the White Peak. In 1925, a proposal to drive a new road up Winnats Pass was met with grave concern and the society realised that the defence of the landscape would be down to the efforts of volunteers. Over a decade later, after the society – and others – had made representation to the Minister of Transport, the proposal for the road was finally rejected. In 1961, the society successfully proposed a high-level footpath going up from the proposed Errwood Reservoir, along the Goyt Lane and linking with the footpath from Burbage Edge at the Memorial Bridge. The path can be walked today.

The beautifully produced green signs erected on a stout square post are installed by members of the society's signpost team. The society began erecting the signs in 1905 and there are now hundreds of them, each with its own number. During the Second World War, the signs were removed by the authorities to prevent invaders from finding their way around. On reinstatement some of the signs were difficult to find; the irony, however, was not lost. One sign was located in a barn, another inside a golf club.

It has become popular for walkers to note down the numbers of the signs they pass, a little like the trig pointers

Waterfall Low high on the hill (Walk 37)

who like to visit all the triangulation pillars in an area. The most southerly sign is near Derby; the most northerly near Morecambe Bay.

The society continues their good work started almost 200 years ago. It's a great benefit to all users of the footpath network.

For more information about the society or to make a donation, please visit www.pnfs.org.uk.

Peak District Mountain Rescue Organisation (PDMRO)

Mountain Rescue, another important organization, is a relative newcomer. Within the Peak District and surrounding areas there are seven Mountain Rescue Teams in operation, along with the Derbyshire Cave Rescue Organisation, Mountain Rescue Search Dogs England and Oldham Mountain Rescue Team Search Dogs. The Peak District is one of the busiest areas for operations in Britain, predominantly due to the number of visitors the area receives. Growing out of tragedy, the teams are highly skilled and equipped for what they do, be that finding lost walkers, rescuing the injured, or anything you can think of in between.

The purpose of the PDMRO is the provision of Mountain Rescue services within the area. The formation of the teams, as is generally the case in such organisations, is a product of accidents and tragedy. A climbing accident in 1928 from Laddow Rocks near Crowden, where a stretcher had to be fashioned out of a farm gate, and help sought from passing walkers and climbers, is seen as the point where it was decided specialist equipment was required to recover injured people from hill locations. Then two children aged 7 and 11 were lost from the centre of Glossop in the winter of 1962. They were found dead four days later on Featherbed Moss. The search was hampered by the lack of a co-ordinated, organised effort to find the children. Similarly, the search for two climbers who lost their lives after an avalanche on Wilderness Gully in the Chew Valley was hampered by the lack of an organised response. It was recognised that a co-ordinated response to mountain accidents was needed.

By 1964 the well-established winter walking event known as the Four Inns (from the former Isle of Skye Inn near Holmfirth to the Cat and Fiddle Inn above Buxton, passing the Snake Inn and the Nag's Head Inn) had gained a great deal of popularity with a large number of teams from Scout groups. With worsening weather, competitors found themselves off the route and down in Alport Dale, between Bleaklow and Kinder Scout. Some managed to raise the alarm that a terrible situation was unfolding and gradually people were sent to help. But the weather hampered rescue and the lack of a means of communication between rescuers made the task all the more difficult. Three young men lost their lives. A report produced later noted that, had the competitors been better equipped and conversant with the effects of hypothermia, their chances of survival would have improved. It also

Search dog Scout looks after the Mountain Rescue Land Rover while attending a Peak District callout

noted that rescue services should be sufficiently organised to help stricken people quickly and to save life in the case of a large-scale incident. The report was timely, but moves were already afoot to develop a rescue service that could respond.

Today the seven Peak District teams co-ordinate their efforts to help people in distress. Equipment has been developed and continues to be improved. The use of technology, such as SARLOC that can locate a mobile phone from a text message, has meant that the response time for lost or injured people is much reduced. The teams include search dogs, drone units, water sections, advanced medical aid, and experts in search and rescue techniques. All members of Mountain Rescue are volunteers, and the teams are funded almost entirely by public donation. Average running costs of each team amount to between £30,000 and £80,000. Within the seven teams, there are some 350 full-time team members. Members are drawn from all walks of life and are on call 24 hours per day, 365 days per year. Whatever the incident, Mountain Rescue will attend if the circumstances warrant and are suitable for a Mountain Rescue response.

If you think the assistance of Mountain Rescue is required, call 999 and ask for Police/Mountain Rescue. State your position and status. Do not move from your position unless life is in imminent danger.

LOCAL COMMUNITIES

The western side of the White Peak is bordered by some significant towns. Leek, once the centre of silk production, is now a launch pad for many of the walks and activities that can be found in the area. And, of course, Buxton, the jewel in the crown, not only provides some of the most beautiful buildings – the Crescent, being the most recent to be wonderfully restored – but also a thriving arts and entertainment community. In between the two are numerous villages and hamlets that are hidden away but are a delight to explore. In the north is the tourist honey pot of Castleton; on a sunny summer day it is crammed with people wanting to explore the caves and the surrounding countryside.

LOCAL SERVICES, VISITOR CENTRES AND TRANSPORT

Connections from the south and west into the western White Peak are easier and more plentiful than those from the north and east. The towns of Leek, Macclesfield, and Buxton are well served by road and rail. Details of transport can be found at www.peak district.gov.uk/visiting/publictransport.

Numerous accommodation options are available, from camping to hostels, B&B and hotels. There is no wild camping allowed within the area. Details of accommodation can be found at www.visitpeakdistrict. com/accommodation.

John Carr's Buxton Crescent (Walk 8)

The Peak District National Park visitor centre is situated in the centre of Castleton: www.peakdistrict.gov.uk/visiting/visitor-centres/castleton.

THE WALKS

When I set out the way to cover the whole of the Peak District, it became obvious that I should base it on the Ordnance Survey maps. For the White Peak, that is OS Explorer OL24. For this volume, the western sheet covers most of the walks, with a notable exception, that of the two walks in Castleton, which can be found on the Dark Peak Ordnance Survey map OL1. Castleton has been included because it forms the northern gateway to the limestone White Peak and sits directly between the limestone of this book and the gritstone of the first volume *Dark Peak Walks*.

Walking in the Peak District – White Peak West often groups three walks that are centred around one place: a short half-day walk; a longer day walk, where time can be taken to visit points of interest; and a longer full day, that can be both challenging and enjoyable. Many of the walks have been designed to link together, giving the option of a shorter day with plenty of interesting diversions, or a full day linking two walks and providing a good stretch of the legs. I hope this proves useful. A good proportion of the walks will, I hope, be new,

23

taking in areas and points of interest that would not normally be found in a walking guide of the White Peak. This came about because, having looked at the map and seen the potential for walks outside the Peak District National Park boundary, I made a conscious decision to stray into some more urban landscapes. A good example is the walk from Bollington to Swanscoe (Walk 5) that takes in a wonderful apple orchard and a prominent feature, White Nancy, ending with a visit to the delightful canalside restaurants of Bollington. The walk around Buxton is in a similar vein. It is a perambulation around a town full of history and wonderful architecture, with a wealth cafés, bars and restaurants, that just happens to sit within magnificent countryside.

The walking routes have been designed to provide enjoyment, surprise and perhaps some new vistas. I think that walking is more than a period of time spent getting from point A to point B. We should be having all our senses engaged by what we see and pass by during our journey. To that end the walks follow a specific route for a purpose.

For instance, the Castleton to Mam Tor route (Walk 1) takes you past the Odin Mine and its rock-crushing circle, the face of Mam Tor a flamboyant orange in the sun. Set off in the early morning and you can experience the sun rising from the east as you sit atop Mam Tor watching the Hope Valley appear out of the night, a cloud inversion gently drifting along the valley. Then head on down the

Paragliders soar away into the Hope Valley (Walk 1)

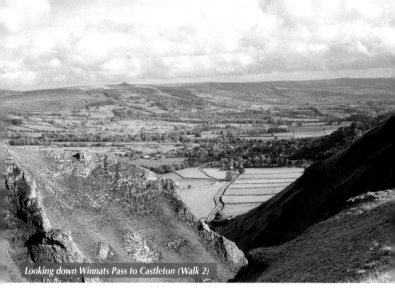

Looking down Winnats Pass to Castleton (Walk 2)

crumpled road below Mam Tor – the power of nature, and gravity, in plain sight – to Blue John mine and maybe a visit to view the wonderful semi-precious stone. After that, it's over to Winnats Head Farm for some magnificent views along Winnats Pass, that become more impressive with each step as you approach. Stand awhile marvelling at how toy-like the cars look in between the towering limestone tors, before setting off for the lung-busting ascent to the top of Winnats. From the top you can sit and rest, enjoying the spectacle of paragliders soaring above your head, then sailing out towards Castleton and on into the Hope Valley, against the late afternoon sunlight. The descent is steep but acceptable, with care, and you get the view of the lonely tree against the grey limestone and, across

the pass, the Norman keep of Peveril Castle. A few final steps and you are down on the road by Speedwell Mine and a boat journey underground. Then you can head into Castleton for a well-earned pint and a meal.

You will also find walks that stray into the areas covered by both *Walking in the Peak District – White Peak East* and *Dark Peak Walks*. I have included these walks to give a taste of what the other areas have to offer, and I hope this proves useful.

Some words of caution on the footpath network. There are at times diversions in place, particularly around farm property. These may be for a variety of reasons. Some signs may indicate a diversion that has long since been removed, but the signs have been forgotten. I have marked the routes using the legal

Walkers enjoy lunch by the wall above Shooter's Clough (Walk 4)

public rights of way or access to open access land. If in any doubt seek advice from the landowner or the relevant Public Rights of Way Council Officer. Secondly, wherever possible I have endeavoured to keep away from roads, but in a landscape heavily used for 2000 years and more, some rights of way and traditional routes have become roads in our modern era. Roads have tended to follow the traditional ways across the land, and many of these also provide routes for walking, either as part of the route, or as a link between two points. Most roads are quiet, and some make for a relaxing change as you can take time to study the wildflowers in the hedgerows without having to keep an eye on the map, as I did when I came out of Brund (Walk 31). But, as always, be vigilant when using roads and aware of traffic.

RESPONSIBLE WALKING

Always follow the countryside code. Close all gates behind you. Do not climb over the drystone walls. Do not light fires. These are the basic instructions we all follow, I am sure. If a walk takes you across open access land it would be well worth checking before setting off that access is available; you can do this at www.openaccess. naturalengland.org.uk.

It is useful to leave a record of the route you are going to walk and the time you expect to return with a responsible person. If you do need emergency assistance dial 999 and ask for police/mountain rescue. Have details of your location at the ready.

Parking can be a problem on busy days. Try at all times to park in designated car parks and do not block the minor roads or field access.

Although many of the walks pass through places where food and drink can be purchased – after all, what better way to complete a walk than with lunch at a country pub – it is always advisable to carry food and drink with you.

MAPS AND NAVIGATION

The best map for the area is the Ordnance Survey White Peak OL24 1:25000. OL1 Dark Peak would also be useful. The Harvey/BMC White Peak 1:40000 has a wealth of information and covers the area well. Smartphone apps are now becoming more prevalent in their use. The GPX files of the walks are available for download from www.cicerone.co.uk/977/GPX.

While signposts, fingerposts and technology are useful, a compass can always ensure you are walking in the right direction.

USING THIS GUIDE

I have split the guide into northern and southern sections. This seemed sensible and again stops the map from flying out of your hand and across the dale. The first walk takes you along the boundary of the White and Dark Peak and gives you a glimpse of the wild northern wilderness for future exploration. The last walk ends at the idyllic Ilam, with its chocolate-box village and beautiful hall. I have placed the dividing line between the two areas at the end of the Pennine range near Upper Hulme.

The walking times are based on traditional methods of calculation. However, when walking in large groups timings can quickly fall to the

Thorpe Cloud and the entrance to Dovedale seen from Musden Grange (Walk 40)

Viator's Bridge, Milldale (Walk 32)

wayside. This is mainly due to stiles: the White Peak has thousands of them. Getting a group through can take time, especially when a spring-loaded gate accompanies a squeeze stile. Allow for extra time on the walks if your walking party is large.

Because of the large number of stiles, the walk directions in places are simplified for clarity. For example, you might see an instruction to follow the path across fields SW for 1.2km. Expect to find stiles, lots of them. Telling you to go through 22 individual stiles does not make for interesting reading.

This guide includes an overview map and route summary table; use these along with the walk summary to select a suitable area for the day. The maps that accompany the walks are based on Ordnance Survey 1:50000.

The place names and features marked in bold within the walk descriptions are marked on the map and should be used as an aid to navigation.

Let me issue one word of caution. While the walking is generally gentle with the odd steep ascent or descent, limestone can be treacherous when wet, so take time and care.

GPX tracks

GPX tracks for the routes in this guidebook are available to download free at www.cicerone.co.uk/977/GPX. A GPS device is an excellent aid to navigation, but you should also carry a map and compass and know how to use them. GPX files are provided in good faith, but neither the author nor the publisher accepts responsibility for their accuracy.

NORTHERN SECTION

Windgather Rocks from Pym Chair (Walk 3)

INTRODUCTION

The northern section is characterised by wild moorland that gradually seeps downhill and turns into pasture that leads into dales and the clear waters of streams working their way through the limestone. The walks move from east to west as they work south into the heart of the region and include some areas that can be found in the first volume, *Dark Peak Walks*, but offer different places to explore and vistas to enjoy.

Some walks would not normally appear in a guidebook of the Peak District. Bollington, Rushton Spencer and Lamaload are all places that fall away from the usual routes. I have included them because they form part of the western sheet of the Ordnance Survey White Peak map and, as such, deserve attention. In fact, these walks offered some of the most surprising and enjoyable days out. Some walks are very familiar, but I have tried to offer new perspectives, perhaps starting from a different place so that, as the route unfolds, you may be exposed to little or unseen views. The walk from Shutlingsloe to Chest Hollow (Walk 15) is one that should definitely be completed, if only for the experience of walking across a little-known moor or descending the beautiful trail back to the car.

If you are interested in geology, this section is perhaps the most fascinating. It begins in Castleton, at the very cusp of gritstone and limestone. The walks around Winnats Pass, above the great limestone pinnacles that overlook the gorge, also tread above the caves of Castleton including the unseen Titan, Britain's deepest cave shaft at almost 142 metres.

There is an unusual walk around Buxton (Walk 8). A psychogeographical foray around the town's major sites, one where I encourage you to choose your own route, it makes for a wonderful afternoon of gentle exploration.

The rugged terrain around the Goyt Valley with its moorland views gives a gentler introduction to the Dark Peak than, say, Bleaklow might, and is a good way of establishing whether you would like to explore the wilderness areas of the high moorlands.

Finally, the routes settle down into limestone country and some impressive landscape features such as the Dragon's Back, the limestone reefs of Chrome Hill and Parkhouse. It is here also that the walks start to engage with the older communities of silk weavers, cotton mills, canal systems and the salt and drove roads.

WALK 1
Castleton to Mam Tor

Start/Finish	Castleton SK 147 829
Distance	4.5 miles (7.5km)
Ascent/Descent	415m
Time	3hr
Terrain	Footpaths with some moderate ascent and descent
Map	OS 1:25000 Explorer OL24 and OL1
Refreshments	Castleton
Parking	Castleton car park SK 149 829

The village of Castleton sits on the boundary between the gritstone and peat of the Dark Peak and the limestone and pasture of the White Peak. The village is dominated by the 'Shivering Mountain', Mam Tor with its near-vertical face of shale, and the narrow gorge of Winnats Pass.

Begin the walk on the opposite side of the road to the entrance to **Peak Cavern**. ▶

There are several caves in Castleton to choose from on a rainy day.

Go up the steps; a signpost points to the public footpath that runs by the side of the house. Then go through several gates to cross pasture in a NW direction following **Odin Sitch** upstream. On reaching the drive to **Dunscar Farm**, go straight across and continue over a field until the path veers right; follow it over a concrete bridge then go left through successive gates to a second farm drive. Cross the drive and follow the footpath straight ahead through the gate and up steps then, maintaining your course, continue on to the crushing circle of Odin Mine. ▶

Odin Mine is now closed but the ore-crushing wheel and circle can be seen, and its position gives a sense of the conditions the miners worked in.

Follow the footpath through the mine workings to the road and turn right along the roadway.

The road is now closed to traffic due to a massive landslip that continues to this day as Mam Tor shivers

down the valley. It is interesting to see the destructive power of gravity and nature.

Where the road turns sharp left take the footpath on the right down to **Mam Farm**, keeping to the left as you skirt the farm buildings. Shortly after clearing the farm, take the footpath left and ascend into woodland. Where the footpath forks keep left ascending to a wooden stile that leads you onto the bare hillside overlooking Castleton and the Hope Valley. Follow the steadily rising footpath up to The Great Ridge. At the top, go through a gate to arrive at **Hollins Cross**. ▶

Go left and follow the slabbed ridge trail to the summit of **Mam Tor**. From the Ordnance Survey **triangulation pillar**, follow the stone slabs and steps SW down to the road, then go immediately S through a gate and bear left down a field to a second gate leading onto minor road. Turn left along the road, then turn right, into the entrance of the **Blue John Cavern**.

> **Blue John** is a semi-precious mineral known for its purple-blue or yellow colouring. It is now only mined in this hillside and the Blue John and Treak Cliff caverns are the only ones working the seam. The process of turning the mineral into artefacts is long and laborious: first the stone is air dried for a year, then it is sealed with epoxy resin before it can be worked. The name Blue John is said to come from the French *bleu-jaune*, blue-yellow, the colours of the stone.

In the days before Grindsbrook Booth had a church, burials took place at Castleton; the coffin was carried along the 'Coffin Route' over Hollins Cross.

The ore-crushing circle of Odin Mine

Winnats Pass from Winnats Head Farm

Speedwell Cavern is unique among the caves in Castleton in that it is flooded and therefore only accessible by boat.

From the front of the mine entrance go SW through the gate and follow the path to Winnats Head Farm. Go through the gate onto the road and begin to descend Winnats Pass. Stop when you see a wall rising E up the steep hillside on the northern side of the limestone gorge. Ascend the steep hillside. At the top of the hill a gate leads onto the hillside above **Treak Cliff Cavern**; this is a good place for watching paragliders launch themselves into the air.

Walk in an easterly direction across the top of **Winnats** to take in the views of the pass and also the Great Ridge that runs north along the skyline from Mam Tor to Lose Hill. At the end of the limestone gorge, descend to the road by **Speedwell Cavern** and follow the road back into **Castleton**. ◄

WALK 2
Winnats Pass to Cave Dale

Start/Finish	Peak District National Park Visitor Centre, Castleton SK 149 829
Distance	7.5 miles (12km)
Ascent/Descent	450m
Time	3.5hr
Terrain	Footpath, trail, road
Map	OS 1:25000 Explorer OL1 and OL24
Refreshments	Castleton
Parking	Peak District National Park Visitor Centre, Castleton SK 149 829

Two huge limestone gorges to explore has to be a good thing. The first, Winnats Pass, you experience from above; it's a little-used route that requires a good head for heights, as well as strength and stamina. But the rewards are magnificent. The second, Cave Dale, is experienced from the bottom, although there is a path on the private land along the top that can, if permission is sought, give incredible views of Peveril Castle and Cave Dale.

This walk has steep ascents and descents along often wet and slippery ground. There is also a degree of exposure that some may not be comfortable with. Please ensure that you are able and that the weather conditions are suitable for attempting this route.

From the national park visitor centre, walk W up the **A6187** and enter the car park at **Goosehill Hall** on your left. Cross the car park SE into the centre of **Castleton**. Turn right before the arched stone bridge, passing the access point to **Peak Cavern**, and follow the path through the narrow lane that brings you to the rear of Goosehill Hall. Go through the steel gate behind Goosehill Hall to join the permissive route across the hillside as it goes in a westerly direction towards **Cow Low**. On reaching a drystone wall, pass through a small metal gate and turn

Cars edge their way down the narrow Winnats Pass

immediately left to ascend the steep rocky path that threads its way on the right-hand side of the wall to the top of Long Cliff.

An alternative route after passing through the gate in the drystone wall would be to follow the road up through **Winnats Pass**, keeping to the right side of the gorge and walking along the wide grass verge, until you reach Winnats Head Farm, then re-join the walk route.

◄ At the top, go right and proceed NW along the wall line. Make sure you take in the views of Winnats Pass and take care not to venture too near to the open edge of the rock face. The grass and limestone rock can be very slippery when wet.

Take care as you work your way up and if you're walking with others, leave plenty of room between each other to avoid being hit by a dislodged rock.

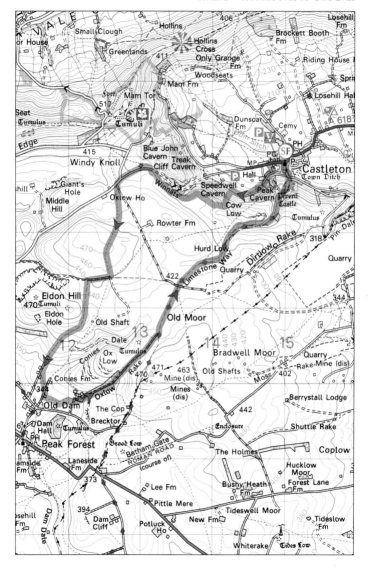

Below your feet is Britain's deepest cave shaft; at a depth of almost 142 metres the shaft is twice as deep as the distance between you and the road running up Winnats Pass. It was named **Titan** and was found in 1999 after being lost since the mid 1700s! Titan has links underground to both Peak Cavern and Speedwell Cavern. It took years to clear a way into the shaft as many of the passages made by miners were blocked. Miners had carved their initials into the tunnel walls and this verified the existence of a route for the modern-day explorers. The length of the cave system is thought to be approaching 12 miles (20km). And all this is right below your feet.

On reaching the road at the top of the pass go left along the carriageway, passing Winnats Head Farm on your right, and proceed to the road junction. Turn left, then take the first left down the farm track. Go immediately right, taking a diagonal line and keeping well to the left of **Oxlow House**, then follow the wall line running generally S over several stiles to reach a wide farm track. Go right for approximately 250 metres then take the bridleway left across open access land until just prior to reaching a small group of trees at the second field boundary on the left. Where the left-hand wall begins to sweep SW, go directly W to reach Eldon Hole.

Eldon Hole, a popular pothole for cavers only, offers walkers a glimpse into the often, dark arts of caving from the safety of solid grass pasture. The cave is 55 metres deep and extremely wet and slippery. As with all the caves and mines in the area, do not attempt to enter: they can be extremely dangerous and rockfalls and flooding are common.

Follow the wall line S from Eldon Hole until you meet a wall running E. Follow this until you reach the bridleway again, then turn right down the track, passing the farm to gain the footpath on the left just prior to a small stone shed. Cross the fields going S to a minor

lane leading to **Conies Farm**. Turn right along the lane. Just after passing a house, go through the gate on the left and take the footpath across fields, initially SE then NE, to arrive at a house driveway. Go straight across and take the bridleway up through **Oxlow Rake** eventually arriving at the junction with the Limestone Way. Go left, following the **Limestone Way** NE, passing **Hurd Low** on your left, to arrive at the entrance to Cave Dale.

Cave Dale in early spring

CAVE DALE

Cave Dale is a beautiful limestone gorge, its sides lined with grass slopes and flecked with limestone outcrops. The dale presented a problem for the Normans when they arrived in the area. The significant lead and silver deposits and the wood contained in the Peak Forest meant that it was prized land and needed to be protected. So the Keeper of the Forest, William Peveril, decided to place a castle on the rocky promontory soon after the Normans conquered England. The village of Castleton was established a century after the castle was built. The keep that is seen today was built by King Henry II after the Peverils lost control, having backed the wrong side against the king's family. In the centuries that followed, the castle fell into ruin and its fortunes were only revived after Sir Walter Scott published *Peveril of the Peak*. Much later, the mass trespass on nearby Kinder Scout kindled the flames of the now-burgeoning outdoor walking movement and, with all the new walkers and visitors to the area taking an interest in this strange structure perched high above the dark chasm, the castle's future was secured.

Peveril Castle from the top of Cave Dale

Descend the dale through the gate and emerge below Peveril Castle back into **Castleton**. Go left then right, circling the village green, then continue down to the main road and turn left to return to the visitor centre.

WALK 3
Windgather Rocks

Start/Finish	Errwood Reservoir car park SK 013 756
Distance	6.5 miles (10.5km)
Ascent/Descent	400m
Time	3.5hr
Terrain	Footpath, trail, road
Map	OS 1:25000 Explorer OL24
Refreshments	N/A
Parking	Errwood Reservoir car park SK 013 756

This is a lovely walk along forest trails and gritstone edges. Being so close to the road, Windgather Rocks is a popular climbing crag. It is rare a day goes by without some climbing activity that provides a few moments of entertainment and wonder while having a brew. The return down Foxlow Edge is one of the secrets of this part of the White Peak and makes for a wonderfully pleasing end to the walk.

From the car park, walk NW up The Street – the old Roman road – until the open pasture on your right ends and you arrive at a gate leading into the forest on your right. ▶

Go through the gate and follow the trail N until you leave the forest through a gate at **Oldfield**. Walk straight on to Oldfield Farm and along the farm track, leaving the farmyard by a gate. Continue N along the track, passing through a second gate leading you past the farm buildings at **Normanwood**. At the far end of the buildings go through another gate and descend the lane. Follow it as it swings right to a stile leading into a field. Go over the stile and cross the field, leaving by a gate onto a farm track. Turn left, walking down the track, through a gate at the bottom and across a stream, then ascend the other side.

If walking in autumn, early morning as the sun is rising is a good time to see a cloud inversion in the Goyt Valley from the entrance to the forest.

At the steel farm gate across the track, bear left after the gate up a steep lane hedged on both sides. At the top follow the lane left, passing across the cattle grid by **Overton Hall Farm**. At the end of the lane, cross the road and ascend the rough moorland opposite. As you crest the hill, bear right to cross a stile in the stone wall and follow the wall line NW. Look out for a wooden gate in the wall on your left. Go through and turn immediately right, along the wall, then through a gate. Bear left after the gate, passing by a short wall, and walk S up the visible depression of a track towards **Windgather Rocks**. Go through a gap in the wall and continue along the top of the rocks until you exit via a wooden gate.

Windgather Rocks sits on the border of Cheshire and Derbyshire and gives fine views across the Cheshire Plain. The rocks are an important climbing venue, being one of the first to have routes catalogued in a guidebook for climbers. Its proximity to the road – climbers are for an easier life if not for one without the frisson of excitement – means that it is a popular venue for the all-important Christmas-day climb. Christmas Buttress has several

Scout on Windgather Rocks

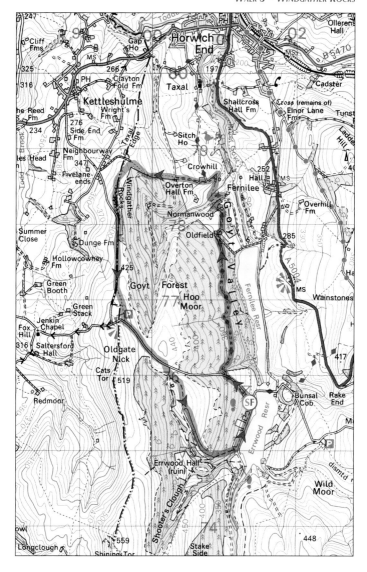

routes on the theme, including Christmas Nose, Arete and Slab. There is also the route called Two Fingers, and perhaps this relates to an unwanted present received earlier that morning.

Continue S following the line of the wall and keeping **Goyt Forest** on your left in the distance. On reaching a signpost pointing SE, go left and follow the footpath across boggy land to Pym Chair. Turn left at the road and walk down, keeping to the left-hand grass verge for safety. After 800 metres cross the road to a layby on the right-hand side and go through the access gate onto moorland. Proceed onto the moor. Where the path forks, go left up a small hill. At the top bear right along the tumble of walls and follow the short marker posts through the remnants of the wall. Follow a wall line SSE down Foxlow Edge. As you come to woodland, bear left at the corner of the trees and continue along the path as it descends through the trees to **Shooter's Clough Bridge**. Turn left at the bridge and walk back along the road to the car park at **Errwood Reservoir**.

The packhorse bridge across the River Goyt, re-sited when the Errwood Reservoir was filled

WALK 4
Goyt Valley

Start/Finish	Shallcross Layby, Whaley Bridge, A5004 SK 008 798
Distance	12.5 miles (20km)
Ascent/Descent	690m
Time	6hr
Terrain	Footpath, trails, road
Map	OS 1:25000 Explorer OL24
Refreshments	Whaley Bridge
Parking	Shallcross Layby, Whaley Bridge, A5004 SK 008 798

This is a relaxing walk, even with the hill climb in the central section of the route. It follows the River Goyt from the outskirts of Whaley Bridge, past the reservoirs made by the dammed river, then high up onto the moors. The return through forests and ruins adds some interesting variety. The walk passes by the beautiful church at Taxal before ending across the ford on the River Goyt.

From the layby on the **A5004**, below **Shallcross Hall Farm**, take the restricted bridleway downhill until it is intersected by another path. Go left through the gate and follow the woodland trail S exiting the trees via a gate into open fields. Continue S across the fields, following the river upstream at all times. As you approach the foot of **Fernilee Dam**, go left at the large stone building, then right, following the tarmac service road up to a 'T' junction. Go right and join the dismantled railway bed S along the shore of **Fernilee Reservoir** to the foot of **Errwood Dam**. Keep to the tarmac service road and bear left uphill to reach a minor road on the other side of a steel barrier. Turn left and walk up the road to a small stone toilet block on the left. On the opposite side of the road is a small commemorative plaque celebrating the Cromford and High Peak Railway.

THE CROMFORD AND HIGH PEAK RAILWAY

The Cromford and High Peak Railway was one of the earliest and highest railways to be built in Britain. It was designed to connect the Cromford and Peak Forest canals, which lay at opposite sides of the Peak plateau, giving a rise and fall of over 300 metres. The line was built to carry goods, particularly cotton for the mills in Derbyshire – it was not a passenger line – and the journey took two days to complete. To ascend and descend the hills, steep inclines were built, with winding gear positioned to pull the wagons up. A good example of this can be seen today at Middleton Top, near Cromford (see, *Walking in the Peak District – White Peak East*), with its engine house, winding gear and incline. The Bunsall Incline reached a gradient of 1:7 and must have been a fearful sight to behold as wagons slowly worked their way down. The incline operated until 1892, with the last trains running along the line in 1967. As you walk around this part of the Peak District look out for the remains of the track bed and tunnels, still in evidence on the hillsides today.

Go to the right of the plaque and take the footpath SE through the bracken over **Bunsal Cob**, descending a steep bank through woodland into open ground. Continue straight ahead, crossing a footpath to reach a wide track going SW into woodland. Follow the edge of the forest, keeping the stone wall on your left, then cross open rough ground to join a wide track and walk SE then E along the northern side of a steep valley to its head below **Wild Moor**. Follow the signpost for Goytsclough Quarry by crossing the steel bridge and continuing along the track SW then W. Go through a gate across the track, following as it rises until it turns S, where a fingerpost points to a footpath running SW. Take this path down to cross a bridge, then follow the wall line W. Go through the gap in the wall, it now runs on your left, and follow it S, above the **River Goyt**. The ground here can be very boggy in wet weather. Several duckboard bridges help, but be prepared for muddy boots and legs.

Where the path splits, go right, down to a stone packhorse bridge and cross the river, rising up the opposite bank to a picnic site. ◄

The packhorse bridge, one of four that crossed the River Goyt, was originally located where the Errwood Reservoir is now situated.

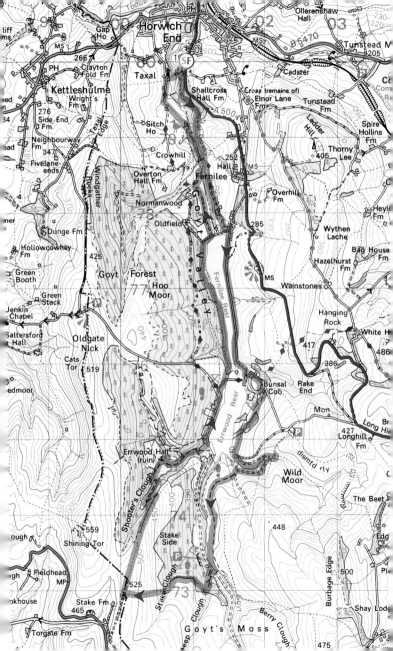

The River Goyt heading downstream towards the Errwood Reservoir

From the picnic site go straight across the tarmac service road and follow the footpath by the stream S as it flows down **Deep Clough**. After a few metres go up the steps on the left-hand side of the waterfalls, then through a gate and along the edge of woodland, the path now above the stream, to reach a bridge further upstream. Go across and ascend the hillside opposite, keeping the fence to your left. Cross a stile and continue along the fence line, this time on your right. Eventually leave the trees on your right as you cross **Stake Clough** and ascend the rising moorland until you reach the ridge overlooking **Stake Farm**. Go over the stile and turn right along the wide track following the signs for Shining Tor. Go through a gate, continuing along the track. Ignore the path to Shining Tor but maintain a NE direction for 1200 metres until you come to a gate in the wall on the left giving access to **Shooter's Clough**. Go through the gate and follow the footpath as it zigzags downhill, eventually fording a stream at the bottom.

Proceed downstream on the NW bank until you reach a signpost on a wide track below a hill. Go straight across and bear right to the grass track sloping up around the hillside to visit the resting places of the Grimshawe family.

It is said that one of **Joe Brown's navigation course locations** is chiselled into stone nearby. The locations give the grid reference, or bearings, to the next location. There are 20 in all. Some have been lost, but many remain as a fitting tribute to Britain's greatest post-war climber. See if you can find it. (Hint…entrance to Errwood Hall.)

Retrace your steps to the bottom of the hill then turn right and follow the path down steps, crossing a bridge then along wooden walkways above the tumbling waters until you arrive at the remains of **Errwood Hall**.

The Goyt Valley held a thriving community with farms, cottages and the grand **Errwood Hall**, the home of the Grimshawe family. The family were industrialists from Manchester who bought the valley in the mid 1800s and lived there into the 20th century, when it was bought by the Stockport

Errwood Reservoir in the mid distance and Kinder Scout on the skyline

Corporation to construct the reservoirs and supply the growing population with water. Close by lay The Street – the Roman road that runs over Pym Chair and alongside the reservoir. The valley was almost engulfed by rhododendrons, planted by the family gardeners, but, as the plant gives little else a chance to thrive, they are now managed intensively to reduce their spread.

From the front door of the hall walk down the stone steps and turn right along the footpath. When it intersects with a wide woodland trail go left and follow the trail through trees to an open area leading to the car park. Go through the car park and turn left along the road, picking up the footpath a little after crossing the bridge. Continue to the **Errwood Dam** and, as the road turns to cross the structure, go straight on down the hillside to the foot of the dam and the bankside footpath.

Follow the path N along the western edge of **Fernilee Reservoir** until you exit via a gate onto a tarmac road. Go right, down to **Fernilee Dam**, but do not cross the dam. Keep to the left of it and proceed along a track until you reach a gate. Turn sharp right, through a gate, taking the public footpath along the concrete drive of a private house, then out onto fields via a second gate. Cross the field to a farm gate then enter a walled lane taking you down to a small bridge with stiles at each end. Cross the lane, then go right, over another stile, then left through a gate to enter a **nature reserve**. The footpath rises through woodland and leaves via a gate into open fields. Cross the fields to reach a tarmac lane and follow this into the village of **Taxal**. ◄

The church tower dates from the 16th century.

Turn right just before the church and follow the steep lane down to the ford over the **River Goyt**. Take the path to the left of the ford, unless you want the thrill of crossing the river on foot, and follow this across the bridge. Go right, then immediately left, up the walled lane to return to the layby on the **A5004**.

WALK 5
Bollington to Swanscoe

Start/Finish	Bollington Recreation Ground SJ 930 780
Distance	7 miles (11km)
Ascent/Descent	230m
Time	3.5hr
Terrain	Footpath, trails, road
Map	OS 1:25000 Explorer OL24
Refreshments	Bollington
Parking	Bollington Recreation Ground SJ 930 780

Walking out of an urban environment into the countryside should be encouraged wherever possible. This walk does exactly that, leaving a bustling town along a trail, then working across the countryside to engage in a fine ridge walk and finishing alongside a wonderful canal. Along the way the route passes a delightful apple orchard, a famous landmark and welcoming canalside cafés.

Starting at the car park of **Bollington Recreation Ground**, take the path through the viaduct arch, then turn right and ascend the long flight of steps to the former train tracks, now Middlewood Way. Turn right and follow the trail until you reach a road, just after passing a stone labyrinth on your left. Cross the road and follow the footpath to the right of the junction opposite. Regain the trail, once you've passed the industrial estate, by descending the wooden ramps, and turn right again to continue along the trail.

Just as power pylons come into view by the trail, turn left before the blue cycle/walkers' sign. Follow the path across the canal bridge and out into a field via a steel kissing gate. Continue along the path and take the first public footpath on the right, SE across fields to a farm track. Go through the kissing gate onto the track

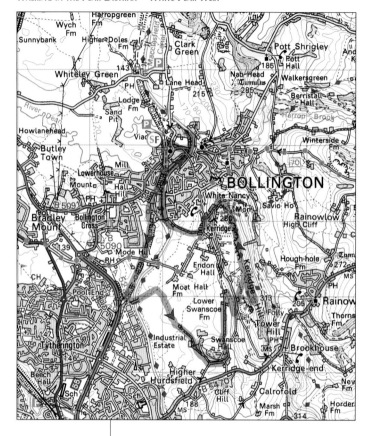

and follow this past a ruined barn to reach a farm gate just after passing the Peak and Northern Footpaths sign No381. Go through the gate then along the track, bearing right through a gate as the track sweeps left. Walk past the apple orchards below **Swanscoe Hall**, then along a tarmac lane to a minor road.

The delightful smell of apples meets you well before you arrive at **The Random Apple Company**,

The smell of apple fills the air even before you reach the Random Apple Company at Swanscoe

where they grow the apples and make the cider. It is a wonderful place to visit, not least because they have many apples that form the heritage of Cheshire apples, with the field opposite the barn full of different varieties, all planted in alphabetical order. The farm sells apple produce and holds a wide variety of craft days for the public.

Turn left at the junction, then bear left a little further on along a private lane. Just before reaching the gates of a house, **Lower Swanscoe Farm**, go right, through a wooden gate and follow the path across fields. Leave by a second wooden gate to ascend wooden steps to a tarmac lane. Go right along the lane, then turn left at the junction, heading uphill to a stone block telling you this is 'Kerridge M+M'. Bear right, through the squeeze stile and proceed along the lane between buildings, through a second gate, then bear right up a steep slope. After passing the gorse, turn right and follow the ridge line S to reach the Ordnance Survey **triangulation pillar** on **Kerridge Hill**.

Retrace your steps from the pillar and follow the footpath N along the Saddle of Kerridge to arrive at the monument **White Nancy**.

White Nancy is a famous landmark overlooking the Cheshire Plain

WHITE NANCY

White Nancy was originally built in the early 19th century as a monument-cum-folly to commemorate the Battle of Waterloo. It is thought to have been named after the lead horse that brought materials up the hill for the monument's construction. The structure is stone, its white coating only added in the early part of the 20th century. In recent years motifs have been added to the white coating, sometimes officially and sometimes by clandestine groups to commemorate events that have taken place. The Olympic rings were added in 2012, with the number 29 added for the gold medals won by the British team. In 2017 a bee was painted on to show solidarity with the people of nearby Manchester following the Arena bombings.

Follow the footpath steps downhill NW from the monument. At the junction with a trail, go left and follow this to a minor road. Turn right and head downhill along the road to a junction. Go left and take the first footpath on the right down a lane. As the lane reaches Bee Cottage, with its ornate gates, bear left and follow the path across the canal bridge, then turn immediately right and descend steps to the canal towpath. Follow the canal N until you reach Clarence Mill. Turn left, leaving the towpath and walk down the track to the road. Go right through the gate into the **Bollington Recreation Ground**, following the path through the park to return to the car park.

WALK 6

Lamaload to Shining Tor

Start/Finish	Lamaload Reservoir SJ 975 753
Distance	8 miles (13km)
Ascent/Descent	555m
Time	4.5hr
Terrain	Footpath, road, moorland
Map	OS 1:25000 Explorer OL24
Refreshments	N/A
Parking	Lamaload Reservoir SJ 975 753

There are two steep ascents to the summit of Shining Tor, a climb that is rewarded by a rest and some stunning views. Having walked along the easy ridge path the route descends the Roman road before heading across country to join the old Cheshire salt routes, meeting again at the unusual Jenkin Chapel. The return to Lamaload through water meadows with views across the Cheshire Plain gives a fitting end to a landscape of moor and pasture.

Turn right out of the **Lamaload Reservoir** car park and walk down the road to a sharp right-hand bend by a road sign for Hooleyhey Lane. Go left through the gate and follow the footpath E along the side of a plantation. As the plantation ends, bear left, keeping to the right-hand side of the wall ahead. Ascend the hillside following the footpath SE crossing three stiles until you arrive at the corner of a tumbled-down wall. Bear right and follow the wall line S, then SSE across open moorland.

> Look out for the **Derbyshire Gritstone** sheep that are a native of these moors. With their distinctive black and white faces, these sheep originated in the hills around the Goyt Valley and were formerly

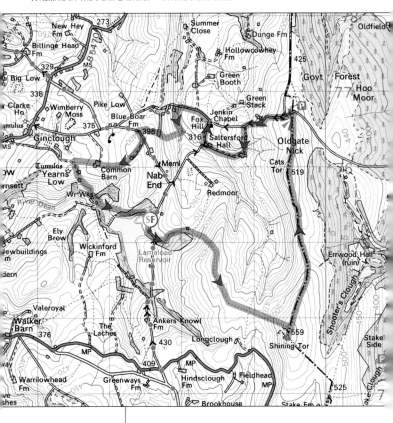

The views from the triangulation pillar are expansive. Shutlinsgloe, Sutton Common and Macclesfield Forest are clearly visible in the SW.

known as Dale O'Goyt sheep. Bred mainly for their meat, Derbyshire Gritstone sheep are among the oldest breeds in upland areas.

After turning SE, cross a stile and ascend the steep hillside to a slabbed path. Turn right and follow the path to the summit of **Shining Tor**. ◄

Retrace your steps down the slabbed path and carry on generally N along the ridge, passing **Cats Tor** and the outcrop of **Oldgate Nick**, to reach the road at Pym Chair.

Go left down the road and take the first public footpath on the left. Follow the track across a stream to arrive at the small collection of buildings at Howlersknowl. Bear right in front of the house, then left between house and barn, exiting the yard through a farm gate. Go immediately right, out onto open pasture and follow the track down to the farm at **Saltersford Hall**. Pass by the farm buildings on your right to reach the bend in a road.

Turn right and walk along the road to **Jenkin Chapel**. After visiting the chapel, cross the road and follow a narrow tarmac lane NW over **Fox Hill**, then descend to the stone bridge over **Todd Brook**. As you reach the bridge go left through the gate and walk across the water meadow towards the stone barn, following the stream initially through trees, then across a stile. At the right-hand corner of the barn, take the footpath right, uphill to a woodland. Enter the wood, turning right to follow a wall up through the trees, emerging at a stile giving access to a field. ▸

Storm clouds gathering on the approach to Oldgate Nick

The views back across the valley to Saltersford Hall, Howlersknowl and Oldgate Nick on the ridge are well worth seeing.

The strange Jenkin Chapel sitting by the Roman road and salt route

SALTERSFORD

The track is one of several ancient routes that pass through Saltersford. The name of the place gives a clue to its most recent use as a salt route, with jaggers – the men who led the packhorse trains – using the route to transport salt from the Cheshire mines on to Derbyshire, Yorkshire and the Midlands. Saltersford Hall is one of the oldest buildings in the area. A date stone on the front of the house says 1593, although the main part of the buildings are later. The roof is made of Kerridge stone from the quarries near Bollington. Jenkin Chapel is situated at the junction of ancient ways. Several salt routes connect here along with the Roman road, called The Street, that descends from Pym Chair into the Goyt Valley. The routes were later used as drove roads for the transport of livestock to market and new pasture. The chapel has an unusual two-storey design with external staircase. Inside, the chapel has box pews for the congregation.

Continue W over fields, crossing three stiles to reach a minor road. Go left, then take the next footpath right, down a farm track to Waggonshaw Farm that sits below Waggonshaw Brow. On reaching the farm buildings go through the farm gate then bear right around the back of the farmhouse, following the concession path, to re-join the track that ascends to a metal gate. Go through the gate and across the field, heading for a large farm straight ahead in the distance. ▶

Go through a metal gate then onto **Common Barn**. Go over the stile in the corner of the stone wall and continue straight ahead, across the yard, passing through three gates into a field. Follow the wall line on your right over the next stile then turn immediately left, eventually meeting a stone track down which you head S, then SE. Pass a low, stone house on the right and go straight forward along a grassy track around the side of a hill towards Lamaload Reservoir. Drop down to a line of houses and cross the stream in front of you. Then bear left up the hill to a stone stile. Go over the stile and turn right following the wall line, then climb over another stile onto a woodland track. Continue along the track, crossing another stile, until you come to a stone building overlooking **Lamaload Reservoir**. Turn right to return to the car park.

This is a fine vantage point for Lamaload Reservoir, Shutlingsloe, the Cheshire Plain and White Nancy.

Lamaload Reservoir with Shutlingsloe on the horizon

WALK 7
Tideswell to Hay Dale

Start/Finish	St John the Baptist Church, Tideswell SK 152 757
Distance	7 miles (11km)
Ascent/Descent	210m
Time	3.5hr
Terrain	Footpath, trail, road
Map	OS 1:25000 Explorer OL24
Refreshments	Tideswell
Parking	Tideswell SK 152 757

Tideswell sits right on the line between E and W of the White Peak. The village is an interesting collection of old houses that tumble down hillsides to the magnificent St John the Baptist Church, known as the Cathedral in the Peak. This walk takes you to Hay Dale, crossing the limestone plateau, to enter this dry limestone dale typical of the Derbyshire dales. Enjoy the relaxing walk and the fine views.

Spend time looking at the community orchard planted with many apple trees that were first established in Derbyshire.

From the gates of St John the Baptist churchyard go W across a parking area then take the second road on the right, Pursglove Road. At the next junction carry straight on through the Market Square, then bear left where the road splits and head uphill. At the top where two minor roads join, go directly W across open ground towards woodland. ◄

Enter the woodland and follow the path W to join a road. After a few metres turn right into a walled lane following it NW to a 'T' junction. Go left and proceed down the walled lane, called Water Lane, until you reach a road. Turn right and follow the **Pennine Bridleway** until you see the signpost for Hay Dale. Turn left here and walk down the walled lane.

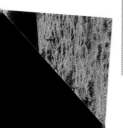

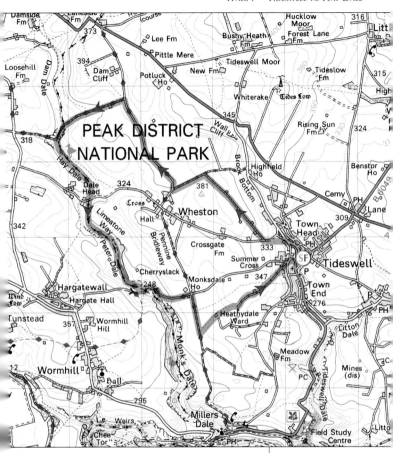

There is an intricate **network of lanes** crossing the limestone plateau and dales. These were used to join communities; provide access to upland grazing; and transport goods and materials such as lead ore from the mining centres. Many are designated for use by all traffic, so care should be taken when walking along them.

Pass the dry **Dam Dale** on your right, a quiet and little-frequented place, and follow the footpath round to the entrance to **Hay Dale**. Cross the stile and proceed down the dale, passing through three gates to reach the road. Cross over and use the stone stile opposite and slightly to your right to enter **Peter Dale**. Maintain a SE direction following the **Limestone Way** through the dale until you leave it via a squeeze stile onto a road, opposite **Monk's Dale**.

Dam Dale, **Hay Dale**, **Peter Dale** and **Monk's Dale** form one long valley running north–south with limestone plateaus on either side. The limestone rock, most easily seen in Peter Dale was formed some 350 million years ago when the area sat under a tropical sea near the equator. What we see today, the wide U-shaped glacial valley, was formed in the last ice age, around 20,000 years ago. With the exception of Monk's Dale, the dales are dry, having no stream running along their length. They are also rich in wildlife, with the early purple orchid and brown argus butterfly generally seen in spring and summer.

Dam Dale, a beautifully secluded dale leading into Hay Dale

Turn left and walk up the road until you reach the crossroads with a house situated in the far left-hand corner by the Pennine Bridleway. Turn right here and walk down the walled lane, keeping to the **Limestone Way**, to take the second footpath running NE. Follow this across the field, over one stone stile, then enter a walled lane, called Slancote Lane, via a small gate. Go straight ahead and follow the lane back into **Tideswell**. At the road turn right, then left at the next junction, then first right, and descend the hill back to the church. ▶

Tideswell Market Square

The views across the rooftops of the cottages towards the church give a sense of how compact the village is.

CATHEDRAL IN THE PEAK

Spend time visiting the church, which took 80 years to build. Construction was held up by the Black Death and the work was finally completed in 1400, hence the two styles of design that are evident in the building, Gothic and Gothic Perpendicular. Inside it is worth seeking out the excellent brasses and tombs. The entrance door to the church has an inscription from Psalm 84: *Quam dilecta tabernacula tua Domine virtutum* (How lovely are thy tabernacles, O Lord of hosts!). The village is a thriving community with plenty of shops, pubs and eateries, most independent, including a baker, butcher and candlestick maker… and Elliott's, probably the best chippy in Derbyshire.

63

WALK 8

Buxton

Start/Finish	St Anne's Well, Buxton SK 058 735
Distance	3.5 miles (6km)
Ascent/Descent	190m
Time	2hr
Terrain	Footpath, road
Map	OS 1:25000 Explorer OL24
Refreshments	Buxton
Parking	Buxton car park SK 063 735

I have placed my own route here as a guide, but I would urge you to explore the town of Buxton randomly and at will. This wonderful spa and market town has seen a renaissance in its fortunes of late. The refurbishment of the Crescent has returned this beautiful building to its rightful position as the focal point of the town centre. Spend time walking around and enjoying the sense of place.

This is the same water you pay good money to Nestlé for and here it is free. Fill up you water bottles before you begin your journey.

The walk begins at St Anne's Well, the outlet for many years of Buxton Water. ◀ From **St Anne's Well**, walk NE along the frontage of the Crescent and cross Terrace Road, bearing to the left of the building in front of you and walking uphill to Buxton Station.

Cross the road and walk SW along the main road with the imposing Palace Hotel above on your right. Turn right at the next junction and walk up Devonshire Road to view the Devonshire Dome.

When it was built, the **Devonshire Dome** was larger than the Pantheon or St Peter's in Rome, or even St Paul's in London. Originally the building was erected as stables for the Duke of Devonshire, who owned and developed Buxton town. It then became a hospital and today is part of Derby University. To appreciate its size and space, a visit

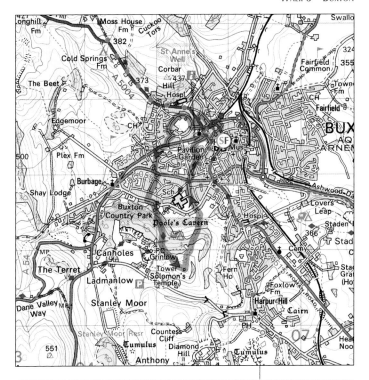

BUXTON STATION

The station was designed by Joseph Paxton, the Duke of Devonshire's head gardener, and also the designer of the Crystal Palace for the 1851 Great Exhibition in London. The fan window that sits at the end of the station platform is all that remains of the original railway station. If you look back to where you crossed the road by the pedestrian crossing, you can see an identical wall on the opposite side of the road; this is all that remains of a second platform that was also part of the station. During the First World War, the station became the final transit point for over 1100 wounded soldiers from the front who were evacuated to the Palace Hotel and Devonshire Dome for treatment of their injuries.

inside the dome is a must. In the centre of the floor a Foucault's Pendulum hangs from the dome and the large bob rotates, scribing the path of the Earth's rotation throughout the day.

Continue up Devonshire Road after the Devonshire Dome and turn left at the junction, then at the next junction left again. Cross the road to enter The Park, a residential area designed by Joseph Paxton, with large villas surrounding a cricket field and pavilion. Walk anticlockwise around The Park, leaving at the SW corner via Park Road onto the **A53**. Go right, past a junction on your right, then cross the road and take the public footpath SW to Macclesfield Road **B5059**. Turn left and cross the road to join the footpath running SW through houses. Cross over two more roads and, at the third road, turn left, cross over and walk up the driveway to **Poole's Cavern**.

The Crescent seen from the Meteorological Station on The Slopes

Poole's Cavern is a large limestone cave, thought to be around two million years old. It is full of stalagmites and stalactites. Water runs through the cave, eroding the calcium limestone. The cave was

mentioned by Daniel Defoe in his *Tour thro' the Whole Island of Great Britain*.

From the cave follow the footpath up to **Solomon's Temple** on Grin Low, and enjoy the fine views it affords across Buxton. Take the footpath heading NE from the tower down the hill, to College Road and follow this until you arrive at **Pavilion Gardens**. Choose one of the many paths that wind through these ornamental gardens full of flowerbeds and ponds, and head for the pavilion at the northern side of the park. Head E across the front of the pavilion and leave by the park's gated entrance, then turn left to view the Opera House. ▶

If you frequent London parks you may feel a sense of familiarity. The Pavilion Gardens, designed by Joseph Paxton, are laid out along the lines of the Serpentine, in Hyde Park.

There are not that many opera houses in the north of England and few as beautiful as this Frank Matcham creation. He designed the London Palladium and the London Coliseum. Today **Buxton Opera House** hosts all kinds of events, including talks, shows, opera and theatre. An original Victorian Penfold pillar box stands opposite the entrance.

Turn right from the pillar box and follow the road round to return to the start of the walk and the beautiful Buxton Crescent.

BUXTON CRESCENT

Built in the late 18th century, to a design by John Carr for the Fifth Duke of Devonshire, the Crescent is said to be more beautiful than the one in Bath. The duke wanted Buxton to become a spa town, fashionable at the time and in competition with other spa towns belonging to great landowners. Inside, the building had a hotel, spa and assembly rooms. The building fell into disrepair in the 1980s and was brought back to life by various agencies, both local and national, at a total cost of almost £70 million. Today Buxton Crescent is the centrepiece of the town and can once again form the bustling hub of the community.

WALK 9
Buxton to Castle Naze

Start/Finish	Lightwood Road, Buxton SK 057 744
Distance	8.5 miles (13.5km)
Ascent/Descent	385m
Time	4hr
Terrain	Footpath, moorland, road
Map	OS 1:25000 Explorer OL24
Refreshments	Buxton
Parking	Lightwood Road SK 057 744

Castle Naze on Combs Moss is generally only seen from a distance. Yet this small area of gritstone and moor gives one of the best circumnavigations of a moorland plateau in the Peak District. It is much shorter than its more famous neighbour across the valley, Kinder Scout, and the views, some say, are much better. The edge path is easy walking but does have some exposure, so tread carefully.

Walk up Lightwood Road as it climbs NW out of **Buxton** and continue along the track through the grounds of the water works. After passing a large stone building, go right where the path forks, and follow it alongside the remains of a small reservoir to cross a wooden footbridge. Follow the footpath up the hillside to a wooden stile in the fence.

Cross and turn right, heading SE along **Black Edge** of **Combs Moss**. After passing the **triangulation pillar** and **Hob Tor**, the path turns NW along the aptly named **Short Edge** towards **Castle Naze**.

Cross the stile in the NE corner and follow the path along the outer edge of the fort. Stay on the outer side of the boundary wall as you progress anticlockwise around the perimeter of Combs Moss. Cross Pyegreave Brook that flows down to **Pye Greave Farm**, below you on your

The ramparts of the Brigantine Iron Age fort of Castle Naze

CASTLE NAZE

The ramparts of the Brigantine Iron Age promontory fortress on the south-eastern edge of the fort contain one of the three entrances. The two ramparts and associated ditches protected the fort from attack across land. The main entrance sits at the prow of the fort and is protected by the crag face. A second entrance is situated at the north-eastern corner where the stile is situated. A third entrance cuts through the ramparts and this possibly indicates it is a much later addition and not a part of the defensive features of the fort. The fort forms a clearly defined arrowhead, giving excellent views from all approaches.

The cabin that has a locked door is for the paying guests; the one with no door and open to the elements is for the beaters and staff.

right, and continue the anticlockwise traverse of the edge until you descend onto a shooting track. Follow the track SW, crossing two more streams and with the boundary wall now between you and the edge. Pass the shooting cabins. ◀ Keep following the wall along **Combs Edge** until you reach a junction with another wall above the **White Hall Centre of Outdoor Pursuits**.

The **White Hall Centre** is famous for the instructors that once worked there. They included some of the greatest names in British mountaineering such as Joe Brown and Doug Scott, the first British climber to summit Everest.

The shooting cabins looking out towards Whaley Bridge

Follow the wall SE now until you pass above **Moss House Farm**, then bear NE for a few metres until you come to a gap in the wall covered by a moveable steel fence. Go right, through the gap and follow the wall line S downhill, taking care on the descent around **Cuckoo Tors**. Continue downhill to pass through a narrow gap between walls, then bear left towards the triangulation pillar and the cross on **Corbar Hill**. From the **triangulation pillar** go over a wooden stile and follow the footpath first NE then SW, until you are below the cross. Turn left over the stile in the wall and proceed straight ahead down the field to a gate leading into woodland. Take the woodland trail straight in front of you down through the trees. Leave Corbar Wood onto a road, walk down to the junction and turn left along the road to return to Lightwood Road at the next junction.

WALK 10
Burbage to the Goyt Valley

Start/Finish	Macclesfield Old Road, Burbage SK 035 723
Distance	6 miles (10km)
Ascent/Descent	405m
Time	3.5hr
Terrain	Footpath, moorland, road
Map	OS 1:25000 Explorer OL24
Refreshments	Buxton
Parking	Macclesfield Old Road SK 035 723

The walk begins on the old road to Macclesfield. It seems incredible now, as you walk along the rubble surface of the track, but this was once a regular route for patients from Buxton Spa to the Cat and Fiddle public house high up on the moor. This route takes you across open moorland overlooking the Goyt Valley and then returns along the track bed of the Cromford and High Peak Railway.

Start from Macclesfield Old Road in **Burbage**, where the tarmac ends and the rough surface begins, and proceed, generally W, along the track. Almost immediately the old railway line comes into view below you on the left. Continue W until you reach the high point of the track, and a gate and stile give you access to the moors on your right. Cross the stile and follow the path, N, through heather until you come to a signpost at the intersection with another path. Go left, W, following the sign for **Berry Clough**, and follow the stream downhill into the **Goyt Valley**. ◄

Note the waterfalls and pools in the stream, with some perfect locations for a spot of swimming.

As you turn N into the Goyt Valley, and just before reaching the footbridge ahead of you, bear right up the steep side of **Goyt's Moss**, and follow the faint path uphill through the bracken. Maintain a northerly direction across the western edge of Goyt's Moss, but take care to

keep on the correct bearing as the path can become indistinct at times, a fairly common occurrence in moorland walking. A compass may well prove useful here to stop you wandering too far from the route. On reaching a wall junction, with a grouse butt on the left, go right along the wall line as it rises up the moor. Cross the steep-sided clough, ascending wooden steps on the eastern side and

73

There are good views here of Foxlow Edge, Shooter's Clough and the Goyt Valley reservoirs.

proceed uphill until you reach a vehicle-turning circle. Bear NE and take the path that follows the wall line. ◀

Descend the steep hillside of **Wild Moor**, exiting through a gate to reach a wide track. Take care as the steep path can be very slippery in wet weather. Turn right along the track, cross a steel bridge over Wildmoorstone Brook, then go immediately right along a wooden walkway, following the brook upstream. Continue along the path to the first clough on your left, then follow the signpost left, uphill to Goyt's Lane until you arrive at a small car park. Go right, and follow the wide, level bed of the **dismantled railway** of the former Cromford and High Peak Railway.

THE CROMFORD AND HIGH PEAK RAILWAY

This section of the dismantled railway line was one of the flattest stretches of the whole journey. After climbing up the 1:7 gradients from Bunsall – below to your left – it must have been a relief to have reached level ground. The line runs across the moorland hillsides, disappearing every now and again into tunnels that were blasted through the hill. Sadly, these tunnels are now closed, but their entrances can still be viewed and their resonance is felt in nearby locations that have been named after them, such as Tunnel Farm, passed later in the walk. The line ran from High Peak Junction to Whaley Bridge, connecting the Cromford and Peak Forest canals, with branches off to outlying places, including one that ran into Buxton Station.

Walk SE along the dismantled track bed, enjoying the views and the easy walking. Eventually you will arrive at a blocked-up tunnel entrance. Go left just before reaching the tunnel, taking the signposted footpath, E, up and over the hill and descending to a gate leading into woodland. Follow the woodland path as it zigzags down through the trees, eventually descending steps onto a tarmac lane. Go right and walk down the lane through **Edgemoor** until just after a pair of stone gateposts by Plex Lodge. Turn right and walk up the road until you reach **Plex Farm**. Then go left across the stile and through the yard to exit via a wooden stile into

fields. Continue straight ahead to cross a stile; the path leads directly into woodland.

Follow the clear woodland path S and exit over a stone stile into open fields. Keep going S, passing through a wooden gate to reach farm buildings. After going past the first building, turn left across the front of the house, following the public footpath through a steel gate to head down fields, SE, crossing a wooden stile and a further field, before exiting via a gate onto a driveway. Turn right, go through the squeeze stile to the left of the gate, then turn right and walk up Macclesfield Old Road and return to the start of the walk in **Burbage**.

The view towards the Goyt Valley from the dismantled railway

WALK 11
Millers Dale to Wormhill

Start/Finish	Millers Dale Station Ranger Centre SK 138 732
Distance	7 miles (11km)
Ascent/Descent	400m
Time	3.5hr
Terrain	Footpath, trails, road
Map	OS 1:25000 Explorer OL24
Refreshments	Millers Dale Station Ranger Centre
Parking	Millers Dale Station Ranger Centre SK 138 732

Spend time on this walk exploring nature in Monk's Dale. The very local environment of a damp and shaded dale has encouraged a wide variety of plant life. The walk follows the old trails left by the monks of Lenton Priory, then sweeps across the limestone plateau to the wonderful village of Wormhill, before returning along the Monsal Trail. Limestone can be slippery when wet so take care and time.

From the **Millers Dale Station Ranger Centre** leave the car park by the road and turn left up the hill. At the first bend, take the footpath on the right and, as soon as you have gone through the second gate, turn left towards trees and pick up an old sledway that makes its way down to the stream in **Monk's Dale**. Just before descending to the stepping stones across the stream, turn left and follow the footpath along the hillside, walking upstream to cross a wooden footbridge. Continue N up Monk's Dale keeping to the right-hand side of the stream. ◄

After passing through a small gate the stream will have vanished, its upstream journey now taking place underground.

Carry on along the path until you reach an open field. Maintain the same direction across the field to reach a minor road and exit Monk's Dale.

Monk's Dale is a National Nature Reserve and Site of Special Scientific Interest (SSSI). The yew and

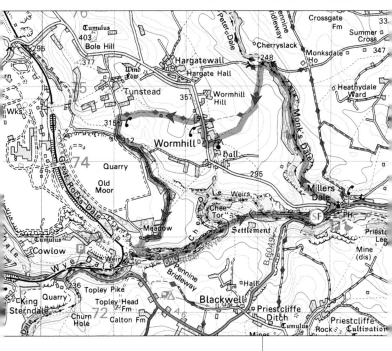

mixed woodland contain the dark red helleborine that loves the damp and shaded conditions, as do the mosses, lichens and fungi that cover the walls and fallen trees.

Turn left along the road for a few metres then take the footpath on the left up the steep hillside and enter a walled green lane via a wooden gate. Follow this SW to a second wooden gate. After going through, take the squeeze stile on the left across fields to another walled lane, then go through a wooden gate into a large square field. Walk along the footpath towards the farm buildings. Enter the yard through the metal farm gate and turn left by the corner of the left-hand building, going over the wooden stile to follow the lane to the church at **Wormhill**.

St Margaret's Church in Wormhill has a tower and roof that are unique in Derbyshire. The corners of the tower are built from Tufa stone, a type of limestone. The strange diamond-shaped roof is known as a Rhenish Helm.

Continue past the church to the road junction and turn right. Walk along the footpath, past James Brindley's memorial and, on your left, the wooden stocks.

In the centre of the village is a memorial to canal builder **James Brindley** who was born close by at Tunstead and who engineered the Bridgewater Canal in Manchester. The construction of what became known locally as the Duke's Big Ditch opened up the route to Manchester for the transport of coal from the Duke of Bridgewater's mines, having a major impact on the economic prosperity of Manchester and the growth of the cotton industry. The memorial also serves as the village well and is dressed every year in late summer.

Keep N along the road until you come to the entrance of Old Hall Farm, opposite. Cross the road and walk through the farmyard to a walled lane crossing fields. Follow the lane until you reach the road at **Tunstead**. Turn left and walk past a small group of houses. Just after the final house, take the footpath left over the stile and walk SE along a field boundary then through a wooden gate. Continue in this direction until you arrive at a double gate, on either side of a lane, by the left of an old dewpond. Go through the first gate and turn right, following the footpath up through the trees, high above Flag Dale. Go over a stile into open ground. Turn left and follow the hedge line through a gate at the corner of two hedges. Then go right, up the field towards trees on the skyline. Cross the stile and go right along a fenced path to reach a tarmac lane.

Turn left and follow the lane, keeping to it as it turns right through Mosley Farm, at **Meadow**. As you leave the

The moss and lichen-covered walls of Monk's Dale

farm buildings, go left, following the marker post downhill, keeping to the zigzag path until you arrive at a signpost pointing the way to the Monsal Trail. Go right here, through the gate and join the trail, turning left to follow it all the way back to **Millers Dale Station**.

THE MONSAL TRAIL

The Monsal Trail was the former rail line that connected Manchester to Matlock. It carried mainly freight, especially limestone from the surrounding quarries of the White Peak. It closed in 1968. This section of the trail passes through several tunnels – some are illuminated during daytime hours – and is popular with cyclists and walkers. A general rule is to maintain a course on the left-hand side of the trail to avoid collision. As you approach Millers Dale Station a giant limekiln can be viewed on the left.

WALK 12
Millers Dale to Deep Dale

Start/Finish	Millers Dale Station Visitor Centre SK 138 732
Distance	11 miles (18km)
Ascent/Descent	635m
Time	6hr
Terrain	Footpath, trails, road
Map	OS 1:25000 Explorer OL24
Refreshments	Millers Dale Station Ranger Centre
Parking	Millers Dale Station Ranger Centre SK 138 732

This walk has so much to offer that it is difficult to highlight the best bits. It starts from the old Millers Dale Station, once the busiest outside London. Next it traverses the limestone plateau to Chelmorton, with its narrow fields, church and pub, and then takes you down a beautiful and secluded dale. The route finishes with a thrilling walk along stepping stones down the deep, narrow gorge of the River Wye.

Note: If the River Wye is in spate it may not be possible to follow the last part of the walk. The path in that section follows stepping stones along the river and these may be below the surface of the water and impassable. The riverside path can also be very slippery on the rocky sections. An alternative route is to take the Monsal Trail from Blackwell Mill cycle centre back to Millers Dale Station.

Note the people abseiling off the viaduct down into Chee Dale.

From **Millers Dale Station** head W along the trail, crossing the viaduct over the River Wye to reach a footpath at the other end on your left. ◀

Go left through the squeeze stile and ascend through woodland then out into open fields. Follow the marker post to cross a stile then step over a stream. Walk up the field, exiting it via a gate onto the **B6049**. Take care on the road. Turn left and, after 80m, cross the road and take the stone track, Long Lane, on the right, uphill. Across

The stepping stones in the River Wye at Chee Dale

Blackwell Dale, to your right, you can see ancient strip lynchets high up on the hillside.

Continue along Long Lane until you reach a minor road. Turn right, walking down the road to pass through **Priestcliffe Ditch**. Just as the houses end by a right-hand bend, go left through a gate and follow the footpath across the fields, initially SW then S to reach the **A6**. Cross the road and go right, along the front of the woodland, then veer left to enter the track, called Senners Lane. Follow this all the way to a minor road, then go straight ahead towards a recycling facility. Turn left to go through a farm gate as you approach the gates of the 'landfill station'. Follow this track S until you come to a minor road, Pillwell Lane, with four marker posts ahead of you.

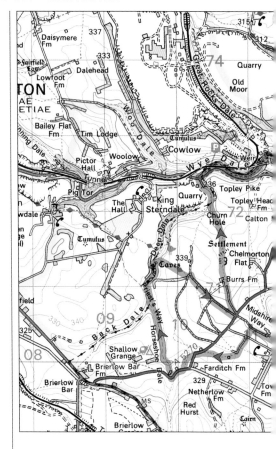

As you begin walking down the lane, just after passing through a gate, a path on the left leads to the **Five Wells Chambered Cairn**. When excavated, the Neolithic chamber – the highest position of any such tomb in Britain – was found to contain the remains of 12 people along with pottery and arrowheads.

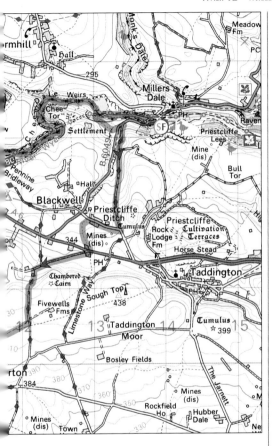

Walking down Pillwell Lane, take the public bridle-way that is first on the right, going through the gate to head SW across fields and through a former lead-mining site known as Grove Rake. Descend into **Chelmorton**, passing on your right the village spring, known locally as the 'Illy Willy Water' to arrive at the church and, facing the congregation, the Church Inn.

CHELMORTON

Remnants of flint tools provide evidence of habitation around Chelmorton that goes back to the Mesolithic period. The village was once situated to the north-west, around Burrs Farm (which you will pass later in the walk). The remains of walls from the Roman settlement can be seen around that area. The name comes from the Norse: originally Ceolmaer's Hill, the hill overlooking the village is now known as Chelmorton Low. The village was settled in Norman times with fields and farms running in line with the local water supply at the foot of Grove Rake, the water running from the spring down the centre of the main street and collecting at the bottom, with all the mud and effluent. Originally the fields would have been larger, but were enclosed during the 12th century, forming the narrow strip fields that are now evident. The drystone walls were added later; originally the field boundaries would have been grass mounds known as 'balkes'. In medieval times the village was the centre of a long-running legal battle between the Cistercian Abbey of Merevale and the Priory of Lenton, who stole the abbey's sheep from the fields in Chelmorton. The legal battle raged on for three centuries, only coming to an end with the Dissolution of the Monasteries.

The Church Inn, Chelmorton

Walk down the hill from the church and at the crossroad turn right following the **Midshires Way** along a track. After passing Shepley Farm on your right, continue along

the track for a further 25 metres then turn left down a walled grassy lane that cuts across several narrow, walled fields from the medieval enclosures. Cross a road, follow the lane around the tight right-hand bend then take the stone stile immediately on the left to cross fields to a small wooded copse. Go through a gate and continue down the walled lane until you come to the **A5270**.

Go left to the next bend then cross the road and walk in between the chevron boards, then through trees to a stone stile. Cross the stile and follow the footpath across the fields back to the road. Turn right along the road, taking care of the traffic, until you reach a sharp hairpin bend. Take the footpath on the right, going N into **Horseshoe Dale** and follow the **Priest's Way**, a remnant of the former monastic landholders. As you enter the dale, look to your right at the two large caves made by the force of water that once flowed down the dale.

Follow the path down into **Deep Dale**, maintaining a generally northern progression until you come to a fence and wooden stile. Cross this into the **Derbyshire Wildlife Nature Reserve** and follow the rocky path until you reach a large **cave** above the path on the right. ▶

After passing the cave, bear right, following a zig-zag path up the steep slope and passing a smaller cave on your right. At the top go through the gate, then walk SE across fields and stiles to a walled lane. Turn left then right at the lane junction to continue along the lane to reach the **A5270**. Go left, then take the footpath shortly after on the left. Proceed N across fields, passing **Burrs Farm** on your left, then descend a wide dale, crossing several stiles to a final wooden stile at the head of **Churn Hole**. Descend the steep bank below Churn Hole cave, taking care on the slippery limestone, then pass the **quarry working** on the left to reach the **A6**. Cross the road into the car park at **Wye Dale**.

Go right, through the car park, then walk along the well-made lane following the **River Wye** downstream. At Blackwell Mill cycle hire centre, cross the bridge on the left then turn right by the end of the row of cottages and continue downstream along the north bank of the river.

Thirst House Cave was excavated in the 19th century and was found to contain many bronze artefacts from the Roman period.

If the river is too high, go back to Blackwell Mill and follow the footpath to the Monsal Trail, turning left along the trail to reach Millers Dale Station.

Where the path splits, the **Pennine Bridleway** going uphill, go right and follow the riverside footpath. At the first viaduct, do not cross the bridge, but go down the steps immediately on the left. Follow the path to reach the first set of stepping stones along the length of the river. ◄

After leaving the stepping stones follow the path across a wooden bridge and under the viaduct, then go back across the river via a second bridge to reach the second set of stepping stones. After successfully negotiating the stones, proceed along the footpath, sometimes on wooden walkways, until you reach wooden steps rising to the left from the base of the viaduct crossed at the beginning of the walk. Ascend the steps and turn left along the trail to return to **Millers Dale Station**.

CHEE DALE

The carboniferous limestone cliffs of Chee Dale rise some 90 metres from the River Wye in an almost continuous vertical line. This has made it a mecca for limestone climbing routes. Some routes use bolts to aid the ascent, while others, such as Dogs Dinner, are free of any devices, testing the skill, courage and strength of the climbers. Dippers are regularly seen, skipping across the rock on the riverbed. The willow warbler is also in evidence in the summer breeding season.

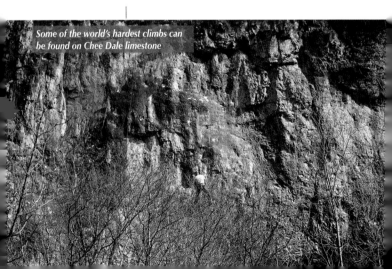

Some of the world's hardest climbs can be found on Chee Dale limestone

WALK 13

Trentabank to Sutton Common

Start/Finish	Trentabank Ranger Centre SJ 961 711
Distance	9.5 miles (15km)
Ascent/Descent	440m
Time	4.5hr
Terrain	Footpath, trails, road
Map	OS 1:25000 Explorer OL24
Refreshments	Trentabank Ranger Centre
Parking	Trentabank Ranger Centre SJ 961 711

Many of the walks around the Cheshire White Peak have views of the large communications mast perched prominently on a hill. The walk from Trentabank has this structure as its objective. It is a gentle route that crosses some of the loveliest farming countryside in the White Peak and visits some secluded and idyllic hamlets.

From the **Trentabank Ranger Centre** car park, head W following the roadside forest trail to a minor road. Cross the road, then bear left along the trail, and W again as it works its way through the forest. After crossing a small dam, the trail ascends a short slope to the left and then exits the trees, giving views of **Ridgegate Reservoir**. Go left here, down the slope to a gate giving access across a small footbridge. Cross and go through the gate opposite, then follow the track NW across two cattle grids. After the second, go left through the steel kissing gate, and walk SW up the fields through three further steel kissing gates to emerge onto a road at **Mosslee Farm**.

Go right and walk into **Langley**. Just as you enter the built-up area, go left and follow the footpath around a fishing pond. Go up the steps at the end, then cross fields in a SW direction, over two stiles, exiting onto the road via a third. Go straight across, walk down the

lane, keeping straight on as you walk beneath a covered
area between houses at **Ridge Hall Farm**. Walk across
the courtyard and turn right at the end of the building,
then follow the path left, then right to a stile. Go over
this stile and a second to enter a large field in Rossen
Dale. Descend the hillside SW crossing over four stiles
and enter a small wooded copse. Follow the path through
the trees, over a stile then proceed to the signpost and
leave the field by a metal kissing gate. Go down the bank
and turn left, following the river upstream.

Leave by a small wooden bridge and cross the road,
bearing left to reach the footpath on the opposite side. Go
through the gate and walk up the fields, below **Foxbank
Farm**, keeping to the boundary fence on your right. At
the top, go over the stile at the right of the field gate and,
keeping to the right-hand boundary, walk uphill, initially
through gorse then open land, to arrive at a double set
of kissing gates. Go through and turn immediately left,

*Looking across Rossen
Dale to Sutton Common*

following the wall uphill. At the top, go through a metal gate and follow the left-hand wall around its corner, then veer right to a gate at the junction of walls. Go through and follow the footpath directly S, across **Croker Hill**. Where the path meets a farm track, keep to the left-hand side of the wall as you ascend towards the communications tower. Go through a wooden gate then a metal gate to maintain course on the left of the stone wall. Exit onto a stone track, directly in front of the mast. Walk up the track and pass the mast now on your right.

> The 72-metre **communications mast** is owned and operated by BT. Originally built for the UK and NATO as part of the Backbone Chain of communications during the Cold War. The tower, and others across the country, were designed to maintain communications in the event of a nuclear strike. It is one of the few communications structures designed to withstand a hit from a nuclear bomb.

Go down the first footpath on the left, passing through Lingerds Farm to follow the path across fields, initially E, then SE, until you reach the **A54**. Turn left, then take the first footpath on the left – the gate is hidden in a hedgerow, so be vigilant. Walk down the field and across the farm drive, then continue in the same direction across the next field. Go through the kissing gate and walk to the right of the ancient hedge along the old drove route. Follow the holloway down to the junction of another path. Go left, following the path to a minor road. Go left again, walking into Higher Pethills hamlet. After passing the ivy-covered cottage on your right, follow the footpath between a stone building and cottage garden, exiting via a gate into a field.

Follow the bridleway, generally N, at one point criss-crossing the stream, until you eventually walk uphill towards **Civit Hills Farm**. Bear right just before the farm and take the footpath below the farm fence, to reach a gate taking you through shrub and out via a wooden gate onto the farm track. Go right to follow the track all the way to the road at **Lowerhouse**. Turn right and cross the road. Then take the first footpath on the left, along the side of a house, and out onto a field. Follow the left-hand field boundary through a gate, crossing a small field to the road. Go left and, as the road rises, go through the gate on the right to a second gate. Follow the waymarked path uphill, turning left through a gate to follow a curving wall to a lane. Go left along the lane, through two gates to a road. Bear right and go over the stile at the opposite side of the road.

Follow the footpath N across fields, until you reach a wooden farm gate in front of a tall leylandii hedge. Go through the gate, then right, following the public footpath round the rear of a house. Go straight across a tarmac lane, following the fingerpost along the Gritstone Trail, through a steel gate and down wooden steps. Cross the minor road and, following the fingerpost opposite, go up the steps and through a gate. Then head directly N, across fields to **Greenbarn**. After passing the barn, leave the field by a gate and go left down the farm track to a house. Follow the footpath right, between the wall and a pond to a stone-slabbed driveway. Go left down the drive, then right down the bank to meet the gate and footbridge crossed at the beginning of the walk. Walk across the bridge and up through the gate on the other side to reach the forest trail returning you to the car park at **Trentabank**.

The tiny hamlet of Higher Pethills

WALK 14

Tegg's Nose to Macclesfield Forest

Start/Finish	Tegg's Nose Country Park SJ 950 732
Distance	8 miles (13km)
Ascent/Descent	555m
Time	4.5hr
Terrain	Footpath, trails, road
Map	OS 1:25000 Explorer OL24
Refreshments	Tegg's Nose Country Park
Parking	Tegg's Nose Country Park SJ 950 732

This is a pleasant amble with spectacular views across the Cheshire Plain and on to the mountains of Wales. At the beginning, the route around Tegg's Nose is a geologist's delight. The walk through Macclesfield Forest is gentle and relaxing, with plenty of places to sit and enjoy the view and a little refreshment. The isolated Forest Chapel must be visited to appreciate its location both in the landscape and the community.

Turn left out of **Tegg's Nose Country Park** car park and follow the well-made path to **Tegg's Nose**. Go through two gates, turning up the steps after the second. Continue on the trail, noting the geology.

The **Chatsworth Grit** includes layers of shale. The rock that was quarried here was formed around 325 million years ago during the carboniferous period. Throughout the site there is evidence of how flowing water formed much of the rock, with sedimentary cross bedding, and ripple marks in the stone formed by a riverbed. Some 20 thousand years ago, Tegg's Nose was encased in ice, and 500 million years ago the ground you are standing on was under the sea.

Just past the quarry machinery, turn right and follow the Geology Trail around the top of deep quarry workings, then ascend a steep hill to take in the views across the Cheshire Plain. ▶

Carry on S descending Tegg's Nose to view the landscape across Langley and the Macclesfield Forest from the **observation point**, then retrace your steps to the main path below the nose and go left through the gate to descend a long flight of steps. Enter and exit woodland

The large radio dish in the middle distance at Jodrell Bank, is the Grade 1 listed, Lovell Telescope, now a UNESCO World Heritage Site.

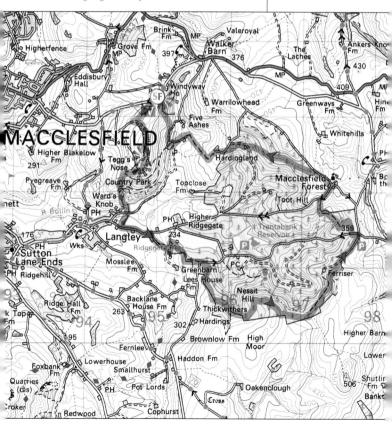

The over 300 million years of geology visible at Tegg's Nose Geology Trail

via two kissing gates and emerge into a car park at the end of Tegg's Nose Reservoir Dam. Cross the dam, then turn left up a lane and immediately right through a gate. Cross the bridge over the spillway and walk across the dam of Bottoms Reservoir, leaving the path through a gate onto Clarke Lane.

Walk past the row of terraced houses and continue along the 'quiet lane', passing the water treatment works on the right. Take the next lane right, walking along it until you reach a cattle grid. Go through the gate on the left of the grid, then bear left along the stone track, passing through a second gate to the left of another cattle grid. Just before reaching a low stone wall on the right, veer left across the grass to a wicket gate giving access into woodland.

Go through the gate, across the wooden footbridge and through a second gate, then ascend the steps to arrive at a stony track. Go right and follow the track across the outflow of **Ridgegate Reservoir**. At the other end, take the right-hand path of the three immediately in front of you, and walk up through woodland, following the path first S, then E along a wall to exit onto a minor road. Go straight on then take the first footpath on the right into **Macclesfield Forest**.

Follow the concession path along the forest track for 1.7 miles (2.8km). As the track turns NW towards **Ferriser**, take the footpath straight ahead across the hillside, re-joining the track 400 metres later, then following it to a gate leading onto a minor road. Go straight across and up the road then turn left into the car park, walking straight ahead and taking the footpath on the right through the gate. Continue along the path initially NW then SW, then NW again through woodland until you reach the corner of a fence and a signpost pointing the way to **Forest Chapel**. Go up the path and out onto the road through the gate. Turn right and follow the road to the chapel that lies just over the brow of the hill.

The Cheshire Plain, Jodrell Bank and the mountains of Wales visible from Macclesfield Forest

THE FOREST CHAPEL

Built in 1673, the Forest Chapel sits wonderfully in the landscape. The simple design adds to rather than detracts from its location between the moor and forest. It is often frequented by walkers and cyclists, and on the first Sunday in June a special service is held, where walkers and cyclists can take part alongside the congregation. The annual Rushbearing Service held in August attracts hundreds of worshippers. The custom of Rushbearing goes back to medieval times when rushes were spread on the floors to keep the dust down and sweeten the air. Over time the act developed into a service and procession with dancing, food and drink.

Return to the end of the car park and turn right, up the unmade track. On reaching the forest, turn left, through the gate and re-enter the forest, following the trail once again through the trees, eventually descending wooden steps to reach a derelict building.

Note the 'JB' over the east-facing window. **James Bullock** lived here and was the father of Walter, who died at Passchendaele during the First World War and was awarded the second highest award for bravery. A small memorial sits at the foot of the wall.

Walk past the left-hand side of the building and continue along the trail until you exit via a gate onto a minor road. Go left until the road ends then bear left along a rough byway open to all traffic and bordered by walls. Take care, as this track is a favourite with trials bikes and, although they are always courteous, it is best to be aware of their possible presence. Follow the track downhill, turning right and then left, and finally crossing a ford before turning left by a farmhouse onto a road. Follow the road downhill and turn right at the junction then, where the road splits by a bench, take the left-hand cobbled track uphill to return to **Tegg's Nose Country Park** car park.

WALK 15

Shutlingsloe to Chest Hollow

Start/Finish	Clough House Farm SJ 987 698
Distance	6.5 miles (10.5km)
Ascent/Descent	445m
Time	4hr
Terrain	Footpath, trails, moor, road
Map	OS 1:25000 Explorer OL24
Refreshments	N/A
Parking	Clough House Farm SJ 987 698

This is such a wonderful walk, with constantly changing scenery and vistas opening up at every turn. It starts with a steep climb up Shutlingsloe, the 'Matterhorn of Cheshire'; the reward from the top is one of the great vistas in the Peak. The section from Chest Hollow to Cumberland Cottage is full of raptors and big skies. If there was a best walk in the book for me, this would be it.

From the car park at **Clough House Farm**, walk S along the lane then enter the farmyard on the right. Go through the gate at the left of the farmhouse and follow the wall line down the field, then cross the bridge and road to reach the lane on the other side. Go over the stile and follow the lane SW until you reach a cattle grid. Go through the gate on the left, then turn sharp right, over the stile to the left of the second cattle grid and follow the farm track until it veers right towards **Shutlingsloe Farm**. Go left here, through the gap in the wall, following the path across the footbridge and through the gate. Ascend a short slope then go through a kissing gate to begin the ascent of **Shutlingsloe**. Follow the clearly defined footpath up the left-hand side of the hill, working your way through the rocks as the path zig-zags to the top.

SHUTLINGSLOE

The name Shutlingsloe is derived from a combination of 'loe', or hill, and that of a local person, often ascribed to someone named 'Scyttels'. 'Loe' stems from the Old English 'hlaw', meaning burial mound. In Scandinavia the word is also used to denote a place where offerings can be given, food for harvest, etc. The area around Shutlingsloe was settled by Danish invaders and the flat top of the hill would certainly have been a prominent place to conduct an offering. The spectacular views from the top stretch across the Cheshire Plain, with Jodrell Bank clearly visible, and Macclesfield Forest, the old hunting grounds, spread out before you. At the foot of the hill stands Wildboarclough. Now a quiet backwater, it claims to have been the place where the last wild boar in the country was killed, in the 17th century. It is worth visiting to see the Old Post Office, a magnificent building that is now a private dwelling.

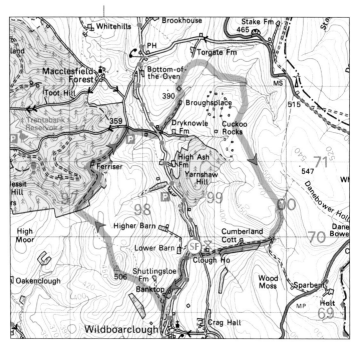

Take the path due N from the **triangulation pillar**, down the steps and across the stile at the foot of the hill. Follow the slabbed path along the wall then left, through the kissing gate, and downhill to the gate leading into **Macclesfield Forest**. Go straight ahead, passing the bench on your left, then turn right and follow the wide forest track NE, passing by the ruins at **Ferriser** along the way, until you reach the road. Walk onto the road and go right, downhill. At the next junction turn left, then right, then left again towards **Broughsplace**.

Follow the tarmac lane across two cattle grids then bear left across the front of the house and enter a narrow lane via a gate. Cross the footbridge and go right to a tumbled-down stone wall. Turn left uphill and follow the walled green lane through the ruins of a farm, bearing right in front of a small rise of stone steps. Follow the wall on your left to a metal gate. Go through the gate and bear right, heading down to a small stream and the rudimentary stone bridge by the fence. Cross the bridge and take the path up a short slope, then go through a wicket gate and follow the marker posts E through a gate to enter Chest Hollow.

Just after passing a stream coming down the opposite bank from the S, turn right through the gate and over a stream, close to a sheepfold. Ascend the left-hand bank S towards **Cuckoo Rocks**.

The moor is one of the few that is little frequented by walkers and gives a sense of isolation and solitude as a result. Buzzards can often be seen quartering the ridge line to the left, at times being harried by crows or rooks. Kestrels and sparrowhawks can also be seen high above the moor, their eyes focused on a pinpoint in the grasses. In the coming years the moor will be planted with a carpet of bell and ling heather, bilberry and cotton grass to go along with the mosses that now form the majority of the surface plants.

There is no defined path across the moor so choose a route that is suitable, keeping to the E side and maintaining a steady general direction to the S then SE. The moor gradually becomes wetter, so skirting the foot of the steep slope to your left is probably the driest option in wet weather. Cross the first tumbled-down wall maintaining a southerly direction, then bear SE, passing through gates at the next boundary to find a grassy shooting track. Follow this SE until you reach a wide stony track by a ford. Cross the ford then go immediately right and take the narrow footpath down to the ruins of a sheepfold. Follow the path downstream to the junction of three tracks. Turn right along the green lane and cross the stile to follow Cumberland Brook downstream, passing **Cumberland Cottage** on your right. ◄

Cross the brook via the wooden bridge and then proceed W, leaving the track onto a road. Go right, then left to return to **Clough House Farm**, walking past the yard to return to the car park.

The left-hand side of Cumberland Cottage is for the guns, giving a little shelter and comfort. The right-hand side, open to the elements, is for the beaters and bereft of niceties.

Shutlingsloe looking down on Cumberland Cottage

WALK 16

Three Shires Head

Start/Finish	Gradbach Mill SJ 993 660
Distance	6 miles (9.5km)
Ascent/Descent	300m
Time	3hr
Terrain	Footpath, trails, fields, road
Map	OS 1:25000 Explorer OL24
Refreshments	Gradbach Mill
Parking	Gradbach SJ 998 662

The bridleway from Burntcliff Top is one of the great delights in this area. As you progress northwards the landscape opens up both ahead and behind giving magnificent views of Shutlingsloe in the N and The Roaches in the S. The walk ends with the waterfalls and pools at Three Shires Head, giving one of the best walks in the Peak District. Combine this with the Lud's Church walk (Walk 18) for a full day.

Walk along the front of Gradbach Mill to cross the bridge over the **River Dane**, go through the gate and ascend the hillside opposite, walking up a walled lane then passing through a wall by a telegraph pole. Turn left and follow the wall line to the corner then turn right uphill to reach a gate. Go through the gate and carry on up the lane to the minor road. Go straight across, keeping to the right of The Eagle and Child at **Burntcliff Top**.

Formerly a public house, **The Eagle and Child** probably takes its name from the Earls of Derby and their connections with the Stanley family, and the landholdings nearby. The name refers to the family crest and the legend of a baby of noble birth that was taken from its home and found alive and cared for in an eagle's nest. The pub was often

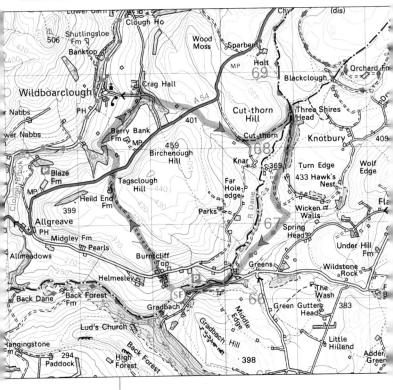

referred to as The Bird and Baby, like the pub in Oxford that is associated with writers such as CS Lewis and JRR Tolkien.

Walk up the farm track and out onto the bridleway. Following it generally NW to Heild End Farm. ◀

As you cross the top of the hill note the magnificent views over to Shutlingsloe. Descend the bridleway to **Heild End Farm** and, as the track sweeps left to the **A54**, take the footpath straight ahead down to the stile. Cross the road and go over the stile opposite, then walk across pasture, aiming for the derelict barn in the trees. At the far

Note the make-up of the bridleway, with the stones of different sizes. Many believe this to be a remnant of a Roman road.

WALK 16 – THREE SHIRES HEAD

end of the barn go left, then over a stone stile, and bear
right across the field to the corner of a tree plantation.
Follow the wall NW to enter a lane. Go right, along the
lane, and then exit via a gate into fields. Follow the right-
hand footpath, straight across the field to the farmhouse
of Firs Farm directly ahead.

Go through the gate and continue along the farm
track to reach the road. Cross the road junction to view
Crag Hall – a rather grand country house with excellent
views – then retrace your steps to the junction and follow
the road SE uphill until it sweeps right. At the bend take
the footpath on the left, following the Peak and Northern
Footpaths Society sign for Three Shire Heads. (Note the
difference in spelling from the OS Map).

Leave the tree-lined track via a gate onto open moorland then follow the path across the moor SE, passing
through a second gate, and across duckboards to exit
the moor via a stile onto the **A54**. Cross the road and go
through the gate opposite to continue SE, crossing a stile
until you reach the minor road at **Cut-thorn**. Go through
the gate and bear right down the hill a few metres then
bear left through the gate and follow the stony track NE to
Three Shires Head.

*Three Shires Head
is the perfect place
for a cooling dip*

Three Shires Head, the meeting point of Cheshire, Derbyshire and Staffordshire, was an important junction for the four packhorse routes. Goods as diverse as silk and coal would cross this point on their way to market or factory. The packhorse bridge stands above Panniers pool. The low walls of the bridge would have allowed horses laden with large heavy panniers on either side of their body to cross unhindered, and to drink water from the deep pool below. The area is popular with tourists, walkers, horse riders and wild swimmers, who delight in the deep pools fed by the small waterfalls.

Cross the bridge then turn right, following the **River Dane** downstream. As the valley opens out take the signposted footpath on the right, below **Turn Edge**. Go through a gate and follow the path SW until you meet a farm track. Go left up the track, then, at the first left-hand bend, follow the small yellow footpath marker right, SE, along a grassy track to a gate in a stone wall. Go through, then straight ahead to a footpath sign. Turn right at the sign, following its directions for **Gradbach**. Go through the gate and straight ahead across the field to the wall corner ahead. Keep to the left-hand side of the wall and follow it all the way to a farm track leading to stables. Go left down to the minor road, then turn right and follow the road downhill until you come to the first footpath sign on the left. Go through the gate and follow the river downstream to a squeeze stile in a wall on the left. Go through the stile, across a footbridge, then turn right along the road to return to Gradbach Mill, bearing right at the entrance, and following the driveway down to the mill complex.

WALK 17
Rushton Spencer to Danebridge

Start/Finish	Rushton Spencer SJ 940 623
Distance	8 miles (12.5km)
Ascent/Descent	310m
Time	4hr
Terrain	Footpath, fields, road
Map	OS 1:25000 Explorer OL24
Refreshments	Rushton Spencer, Wincle
Parking	Rushton Spencer SJ 940 623

This is a beautiful walk over the rolling hills of the Dane Valley. It is a quiet part of the world, so do not be surprised to find few people here. As well as the marvellous views along the way, there's the scenic River Dane filler at Gig Hall; the derelict barn at Dumkins with the bench depicting the Gritstone Trail; and the church at Rushton Bank.

From the junction with the **A523** at **Rushton Spencer**, walk N through the village along Heaton Road. After passing the school, bear right where the road splits, then take the next left, Haddon Lane, crossing the stream and taking the footpath on the right thereafter. Follow the track up through the grounds of the house ahead, then straight ahead up a small field to go through a squeeze stile in a hedge. Go E across fields and three stiles to reach a concrete track. Turn left, then right by some trees and follow the right-hand boundary wall across the field and two stiles to exit onto a tarmac lane on the outskirts of **Heaton**. Go left along the lane to **Heatonlow**. As you approach the farm buildings go right, through the farm gate, to a stone stile at the junction of two walls. Keep to the left of the powerlines to reach the wooden stile, cross, then walk straight ahead down the field, keeping Shutlingsloe on the horizon, as an aiming point. ▶

This is a perfect spot for that photo of Shutlingsloe, showing that it is indeed 'The Matterhorn' of the White Peak.

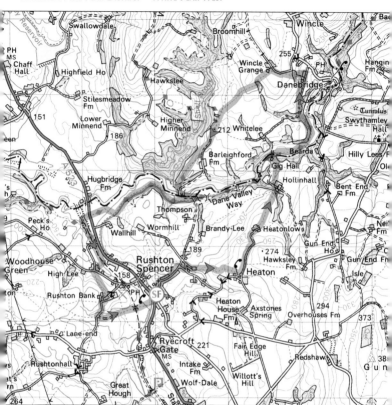

Cross the stile and walk down the hillside on generally the same line to reach a series of steps leading down to a wooden footbridge. Cross the bridge and ascend the opposite steps. After going over the stile turn right and follow the hedge around to the left. On meeting a track, go left, passing the private garden of **Hollinhall**. Just after a barn on your right, turn right, over the stile and then across a field, going over another stile then ahead down wooden steps to yet another stile that leads to **Gig Hall**. Turn right, then left, to cross the bridge in front of the

Shutlingsloe from Heaton Low Farm

filler, for the **River Dane**. At the other side, go right, following the course of the river upstream.

> Here the **River Dane** splits, with a feed taken off to fill Rudyard Reservoir and the river itself heading towards Congleton and eventually ending in the Irish Sea. This is also the border between Staffordshire and Cheshire.

Just before reaching a metal kissing gate, go left, up through a wooden gate into a wood. Walk along the track up the steep hill to the tarmac trail and turn right, following the trail N. After passing a line of red sandstone houses on the left, take the footpath left across the stone stile, up through trees and enter woodland by a wall corner. Follow the markers through the wood, initially left, then up a steep bank, exiting over a stone stile into a field. Go straight on across the field and leave by the gate onto a minor road. Turn left and walk up the road to **Wincle Grange**. Just before the road sweeps right, past Wincle

Grange, take the footpath over the stile on the left. Follow the wall on the right, SW down the field, cross a wooden stile, then bear left to ascend a slope. Bear right, along the wall line until you reach a metal gate. Go through the gate and follow the trees straight ahead to a wooden gate. Go through and descend the path to join the Gritstone Trail after passing through a tall wooden gate.

> The **Gritstone Trail** runs from Disley for 35 miles (56.5km) through Cheshire's Peak District, finishing at Kidsgrove, south of Congleton. Our route joins it at the wonderfully named Dumkins, as it enters an ancient holloway. To the left is a wonderful stone barn, now derelict, but covered with moss and home to a large variety of insects and butterflies. By the barn is a wooden bench, depicting the whole route of the trail.

The beautiful derelict barn by the Gritstone Trail

Go left and follow the Gritstone Trail markers down the holloway, passing a beautiful derelict barn and trail

bench on your right at Dumkins. Leave by a second gate, crossing a narrow patch of rough ground, through another gate, then bear right down the hillside, using a series of wooden footbridges to cross boggy ground and maintaining a SW course all the way. Exit via a metal kissing gate onto tarmac, go right, downhill then cross the bridge over the **River Dane** and then a cattle grid to follow the track up to a stone bridge. Just before crossing the stone bridge, go right, through a wooden kissing gate and follow the Dane Valley Way W along the side of a water conduit. Pass through four sets of gates then leave the trail to follow the footpath on the right down a field, turning left at the lonely stile and exiting onto the **A523**.

Cross the road diagonally left and go through the kissing gate, proceeding straight ahead under the bridge then turning sharp left, over the stile, then up the banking to arrive at the trail along the former rail track that runs to **Rudyard Reservoir**. Go right, along the trail for 650 metres, then take the public footpath on the right, dropping down from the trail, through the gate, across a field and out into the yard of a feed miller. Walk up to the minor road and cross, going diagonally left to a stile hidden in the hedge opposite. Cross the field, heading upwards to the SE corner, then over a stile at the corner of two hedges.

Walk up the field to the fingerpost, then go up the stone steps, cross the private garden, ensuring you keep to the public right of way, and join the driveway on the right of the house, exiting onto a minor road at **Rushton Bank**. Go right and follow the road until you reach the lane for St Lawrence Church. Walk through the churchyard to the exit gate near the eastern boundary. Go right down the field, through a gate, then a second that takes you over the trail again. Follow the footpath downhill, crossing a bridge with a gate at either end, then, keeping the boundary fence on your right, proceed to the stile and exit onto the **A523**. Go right, then left to return to **Rushton Spencer**.

WALK 18
Lud's Church

Start/Finish	Gradbach Mill SJ 993 660
Distance	5.5 miles (9km)
Ascent/Descent	300m
Time	3hr
Terrain	Footpath, trails, fields
Map	OS 1:25000 Explorer OL24
Refreshments	Gradbach Mill
Parking	Gradbach SJ 998 662

This is a wonderful walk, especially in autumn. The paths through the woodland are heavy with the scents of the season and the sound of the river tumbling through the valley. The highlight is Lud's Church, an atmospheric place, full of mystery and myth. The walk back along ancient tracks to Gradbach Mill is a fitting end to a pleasant few hours. The walk can be combined with Three Shires Head walk (Walk 16) for a full day.

At the beginning of the 20th century **Gradbach Mill**, once a silk-weaving mill, fell into disuse. It later became a youth hostel and, after extensive refurbishment, is now a centre for conferences, family and group holidays.

From **Gradbach Mill** head SW following the Peak and Northern Footpaths Society sign No251 for Lud's Church, bearing left as you approach the café to pass through a gate. Follow the footpath until you reach a stone stile. Go over the wall, then follow it downhill to the bridge. Cross the bridge and turn left following the signpost for Roaches. Continue along the path as it climbs away from the river and up the steep woodland. At the top follow the signpost for **Lud's Church** right, until you come to another signpost directing you left. Follow the trail across

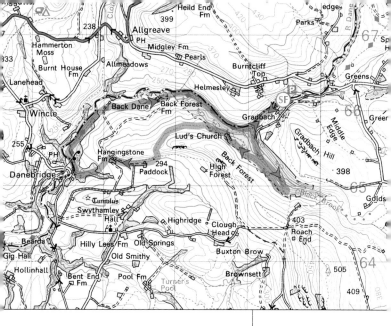

duckboards until you arrive at a rustic fence, guarding the entrance to the chasm. Bear left and look for the steps ahead of you that lead you into the abyss.

LUD'S CHURCH

Geologically, Lud's Church is made of Roaches grit, the same that forms the eponymous edges. It is a chasm, 100 metres long and 20 metres deep, that was created when a landslip occurred along a natural fault line that runs along the gritstone bed. As with many secluded spots, it became a place of worship during times of persecution. The Christian Lollards – 14th-century followers of John Wycliffe, a critic of the Roman Catholic church – held services here. Lud's Church also has literary connections. Many scholars believe the 'Green Chapel' to be the place in which Sir Gawain had his meeting with the Green Knight. This medieval tale of epic chivalry is one of the great Arthurian legends, a hero on a quest, and a test of loyalty and honour. Nature has taken advantage of the cool damp conditions that are always prevalent in the space that has created the perfect environment, and a wealth of plants have made their home in the rock ledges.

Lud's Church

Leave by the northern opening and follow the woodland trail, passing a signpost for Swythamley. The trees are soon left behind, replaced by moorland. Walk along the sandy path through a gate and follow the wall on your right downhill to the junction of trails. Turn right and go through the stone squeeze stile to the left of the gate then follow the footpath down to the junction of three tracks. Turn right and go through the gate below the Hanging Stone, on the hillside above.

> The **Hanging Stone** was so named for the large stone overhanging the outcrop. There are two plaques, one commemorating a faithful dog, and the other in memory of Henry Courtney Brocklehurst of Swythamley Hall, who was killed in battle in the Second World War.

Go along the track, above **Hangingstone Farm**, until a sign instructs no further access, then turn left over the stile and across the field, then over a second stile and head for the corner of woodland. Cross the stile and follow the wide trail through the woods, exiting at the bottom onto a well-made track. Go right and, a little further on, pass through a gate into a broad field. Follow the path to a gate leading into woodland. Go through and immediately left along the duckboards at the side of the fence on the left. Follow the path through the woods, leaving via a stile then continue along the footpath NE until you come to **Back Dane**.

Go right, up the tarmac road and, as it turns sharp right, follow the signpost across the hillside, almost E, crossing two stiles to arrive at the driveway to **Back Forest Farm**. Go straight across the tarmac and along the narrow-fenced footpath, out onto open fields via a stile. Cross the fields and enter woodland over the stile, walking along the footpath as it ascends through the trees and the **River Dane** thunders by below. ▶

At the footpath junction, follow the signpost left down to the river then on to the bridge crossed at the beginning of the walk. Cross the bridge and retrace your steps to **Gradbach Mill**.

There are some excellent wild swimming spots but wait until the path reaches the riverbank and gives safe and easy access.

Heading up the ancient track to Back Dane

WALK 19

The Dragon's Back

Start/Finish	Earl Sterndale SK 089 670
Distance	4.5 miles (7.5km)
Ascent/Descent	430m
Time	3hr
Terrain	Footpath, fields, road
Map	OS 1:25000 Explorer OL24
Refreshments	Earl Sterndale
Parking	Earl Sterndale SK 089 670

Do this walk on a summer evening. It is only short but packs in a huge amount of enjoyment. It should be taken at leisure, the beautiful scenery enjoyed in full. The views from Parkhouse Hill and Chrome Hill are stunning; a real sense of achievement can be had in scaling these hills. Be aware there are steep rocky ascents and descents, so it is not for the faint-hearted, and not to be done in wet weather.

The walk starts and ends at The Quiet Woman public house in **Earl Sterndale**.

> **The Quiet Woman** pub is over 400 years old. The sign depicts the landlord's wife, 'Chattering Charteris', who spoke too much one day and the landlord cut off her head for some peace and quiet.

Go right, in front of the public house, through a gate and straight on between buildings to a wicket gate. Walk across the small enclosure and out into open fields, heading W to a gate in a wall that faces Parkhouse Hill. Descend the hillside using the green track that skirts the NW slope of **Hitter Hill**, exiting via a stile to descend into the final field before reaching the **B5053**. Go straight across the road to the field opposite. Continue in the

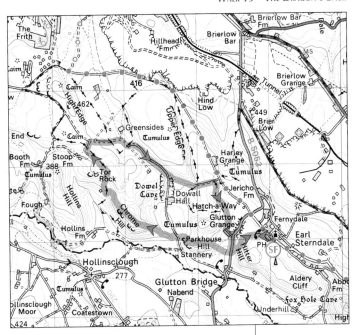

same direction across the field to go through the gate
ahead, then bear right, aiming for the gated access point
to **Parkhouse Hill**.

Those wishing to avoid the ascent of the hill, or
unsure of their capabilities, can bear left after passing
through the gate and follow the footpath around the left
flank of the hill to the cattle grid.

Parkhouse Hill can be taken from either direction, E
or W, as a personal preference. For a W–E traverse, follow
the footpath along the left flank and ascend via the western nose, using the left flank once down to return to the
cattle grid. For the E–W traverse (as shown on the map),
bear right along the foot of the hill and pick up the rough
trod that zigzags its way up the eastern nose. The trod can
be steep at times, so be careful. Once on the summit, rest
and enjoy the view.

Scout on the ridge of Parkhouse Hill

Those with a head for heights and a desire for a little more adventure can proceed ahead and descend the nose.

Go W along the ridge, choosing the route you feel safest with. There are some short steep sections where care needs to be taken. There is nothing wrong in going down on your bum. Two-thirds of the way across, just before the final steep descent to terra firma, there is an escape route to the right, which leads down a wide slope on the N side of the hill to the pasture below. ◄

Parkhouse Hill and **Chrome Hill** are what remain of a carboniferous reef atoll. It is a Site of Special Scientific Interest (SSSI) and therefore nothing should be disturbed or removed from the site. The hills retain their shape which was formed 350 million years ago. Keep an eye out for fossils as the area is rich in crinoids and brachiopods from its time in the tropical seas. The views from the tops are spectacular with Kinder Scout clearly visible.

From the base of the hill, walk to the road and follow NE towards the cattle grid, then take the footpath left just before the grid to ascend Chrome Hill.

Work your way up the SE flank of **Chrome Hill**, the tail of the Dragon's Back, picking a route that is most suitable for you. At the top head NW, again choosing your route across the top, until the descent brings you to the foot of the hill. Exit across the wall. Turn right to follow the concession path uphill, first N, then NE heading around **Tor Rock** until you reach the corner of a wall. Follow the wall NW until you arrive at the farm track leading to **Stoop Farm**. Turn right down the track and then turn right again to descend the quiet country lane through Dowel Dale.

Just before the road turns directly S take the footpath on the left, through the gate and up the steep hillside, then go through the gate at the top. Keep to the left-hand side of the field and follow the boundary wall to a stile by the right of a field gate at a wall junction. Go over the stile and walk down the field on the left-hand side of the wall, then go through the wicket gate on the right. Cross the lane and go over the stile opposite to enter the gloriously name **Hatch-a-way**. Descend the dale to **Glutton Grange** going through the gate into the yard and then left to reach the road. Turn right down the road to retrace your steps via the wicket gate on the left, back over **Hitter Hill** to **Earl Sterndale**.

WALK 20

Flash to Axe Edge

Start/Finish	Flash SK 025 671
Distance	7.5 miles (12km)
Ascent/Descent	440m
Time	4hr
Terrain	Footpath, fields, road
Map	OS 1:25000 Explorer OL24
Refreshments	Flash
Parking	Flash SK 025 671

This is a grand walk. Starting from the village of Flash, high up on the Staffordshire moors, the walk takes in Axe Edge, from which there are stupendous views across the whole of the Peak District. It then descends into the valley of the River Dane to follow the old routes across the junction of the three counties of Derbyshire, Staffordshire and Cheshire.

Flash basks in the glory of being the highest village in Britain and having the highest village pub in Britain too. For such an isolated place it has plenty of amenities including the New Inn, Flash Brewery and a village store. A legend, or myth – you take your pick – tells of the village being the centre of a counterfeiting operation, from where the term 'Flash Money' stems.

From the New Inn public house in the centre of **Flash**, head W along the road, passing the old Methodist Chapel on the right. Take the first footpath right, up a gravel drive, then through a field gate. Turn immediately right and follow the public footpath that runs N between **Wolf Edge** on the left and Oliver Hill on the right. Cross fields and two stone stiles, then a wooden stile onto rough ground. Follow the wall line NE past **Oliver Hill**, crossing a stile,

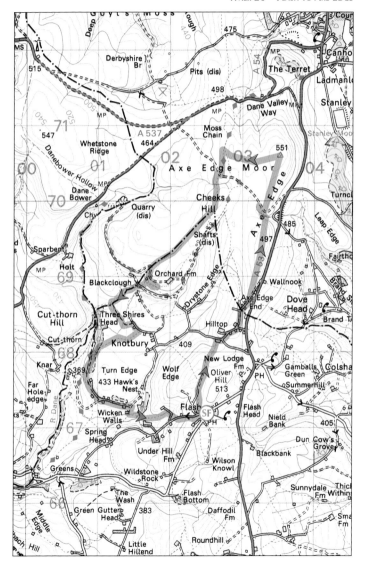

Axe Edge Moor pools provide an important habitat for wildlife

then descending the other side using three stiles to enter the grounds of the farm at Oxenstitch. Keep to the left of the buildings to gain the stile and walk onto the road. Turn right, then left at the next junction and walk uphill to **Hilltop**.

Walk past the terrace of houses and through the metal gate straight ahead, then cross the track and enter the open moorland at **Axe Edge End**. Walk generally N over the summit of **Axe Edge**, then traverse the hillside down to the stream, crossing at the stepping stones. Walk left, up the grassy track onto the road. Turn right, cross the road and enter **Axe Edge Moor** via the access gate. Follow the faint path NE up the moor to reach the Ordnance Survey **triangulation pillar**.

To the left of the fence at the lowest point is the location for the source of the River Dane.

From the pillar, head W, aiming to the left of the rock outcrop that is visible ahead. Walk over the band of rock and down the moorland, maintaining a western course and keeping to the left of the wire fence that runs N–S ahead of you. ◄

After passing the fence and reaching the top of the slope, turn left along the track, following it to the right-hand gate that leads onto the road at Dane Head.

Turn right along the road and after a few metres take the footpath on the left across **Cheeks Hill** to reach the corner of a stone enclosure. Turn right and walk SW down the wide track, passing through a wide gate. Keep to the right-hand side of the wire fence and eventually join the wide track of the Dane Valley Way. Go left through the metal gate and proceed along the wide grassy track, SW. As it turns SE around the hillside take the right-hand track traversing the slope to meet a concrete track. Turn right down the track, then left before the house and cross a stile in the corner of the fence. Walk across the small enclosure and go over another stile then descend a steep hillside down to the river at **Blackclough**.

Follow the track that runs along the right-hand bank of the **River Dane**, then take the left-hand fork, over the stone packhorse bridge, and walk up the packhorse track to reach the road at **Knotbury**.

The Dane Valley, leading down to Gradbach, Lud's Church in the woods and, on the horizon, the hill known as Gun

The **packhorse routes** that criss-cross this area were important trading corridors for the region. Silk from Hollinsclough would be taken to Macclesfield, and coal mined around the area was transported out to the growing industrial conurbations. The geology of this part of the valley is interesting in that it shows a mixture of coal beds, shale beds and gritstone, layered as they were deposited hundreds of millions of years ago.

Go right, up the road, then take the first footpath right over the stile, down the field, keeping the wall on your left. Leave the wall, continuing ahead, then veer right across rough ground to a fenced area. Follow the path through three gates and ascend the hillside to cross a stile. Walk up the moorland and exit via a gate to descend left, down a wooded hillside, using a wide grassy track, beneath a long rocky outcrop. At the bottom join the wide sandy track and follow this left, around the hillside of **Turn Edge**, passing across the front of a house. Keep right where the track splits and go through the gate to join a tarmac road.

Continue until you reach a fingerpost, pointing the way down a concrete and gravel drive to **Wicken Walls**. Keep to the left of the buildings and go through the wicket gate, then turn left along the wall, crossing a field and stile, then straight ahead to descend to the river by the Peak and Northern Footpaths Society sign, No243. Cross the footbridge and ascend the steep bank opposite, go over the stile at the top then bear right up the hillside and walk towards a farm gate. Turn left, following the line of the wall, up the hill, crossing fields through two gates to reach a tarmac lane. Go right and take the first footpath on the left through the gate, ascending the hillside and two further gates to exit onto the road. Turn left and walk up the road to return to **Flash** village.

SOUTHERN SECTION

Ramshaw Rocks (Walk 25)

INTRODUCTION

The southern section has a gentler landscape and one that is more populated. Here you will find some of the oldest landscapes in the Peak District. The walk from Hartington to Pilsbury Castle takes you on a journey through history. Some of the walks have been designed to provide wonderful views. I realise this is a weather-dependent feature, but we can always go another day. The views from Gun, for instance, across the Cheshire Plain and the nearby Bosley Cloud, are definitely worth seeking out. Lunch there, while watching Jodrell Bank turn to the stars, is a unique experience. The relaxing walk down the Caldon Canal, pub ahead and boats quietly gliding by, is not something that immediately springs to mind in the Peak District.

As in the northern section, the walks are arranged east to west, moving south to Ilam. This essentially pastoral landscape does provide some wonderful surprises and the odd frisson of excitement. Dovedale, with its limestone spires and huge caves cut by water, is a magnet for young and old explorers alike. Visit Wolfscote and Biggin dales too to see how they were transformed by glacial action, and admire the wealth of wildflowers that manage to survive on the thin limestone soils.

The gritstone edges of The Roaches and Hen Cloud are steeped in the history of climbing. On any given day you can sit and watch climbers trying their best to grasp that out-of-reach finger hold.

Longnor is a fantastic place to visit. It's worthwhile for the walk to High Wheeldon and the views, for sure, but also for the village itself. Go late in the day and explore the narrow alleyways that are crammed in between the stone houses and shops. This is truly a Dickensian experience.

The southern section ends at Ilam: one man's vision of a perfect society, that today gives us some great walking and an exquisite church to explore.

WALK 21
The Roaches

Start/Finish	The Roaches SK 003 621
Distance	5.5 miles (9km)
Ascent/Descent	375m
Time	3hr
Terrain	Footpath, fields, road
Map	OS 1:25000 Explorer OL24
Refreshments	N/A
Parking	The Roaches SK 003 621

The Roaches is a famous climbing venue where the greats of British climbing hone their skills. The area is full of wildlife; there even used to be wallabies here – some say there still are. Keep an eye out for the peregrine falcons. These magnificent birds nest on the rock shelves on the face of the crag. The views from the top are spectacular, particularly at sunrise or sunset.

Park in one of the lay-bys below The Roaches. Walk SE down the road and take the first footpath on the right through the squeeze stile to **Windygates**. On reaching the farm track go right and follow this through the farmyard, passing the impressive farmhouse on the right, aiming for the wicket gate that leads onto the footpath on the right-hand side of the barn straight ahead. Follow the concrete track out onto open fields and proceed NW along the faint path, crossing several stone walls to arrive at Roach House. The footpath has been diverted to the left. Walk around the perimeter of the garden to gain the wooden stile in the NW boundary.

Cross this stile and go N up the field to **Pheasant's Clough**, following the farm track into the yard, then bearing left through a steel gate, then right, in front of the farmhouse. As the track curves right, uphill, go through the farm gate on the left, and follow the footpath NW

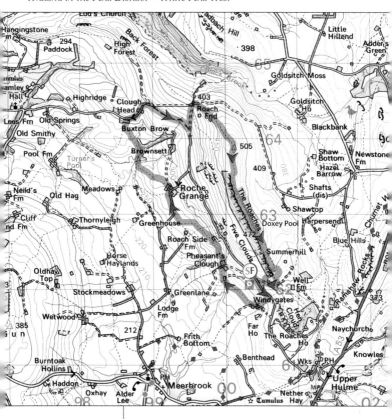

across the field, with the **Five Clouds** of The Roaches
looking down onto your journey.

Cross a wooden stile and work your way through an
area of blackberries in summer, then turn left through
the stile at the end of the path. Cross the hillside eventually reaching a small stable. Keep to the right of the
building going through two gates then straight across the
track and over the stile to enter a lane. Follow the lane
as it swings left, go over a stile and immediately right to
follow the path NW across the fields above **Roach Side**

Farm. Exit via a wooden stile between the end of a hedge and a farm gate onto a minor road. Go right and follow the road into **Roche Grange**.

THE ROACHES

Etymologists will have a field day around this area. The Five Clouds, that sit below The Roaches are a point in case. The word 'cloud' has its root either in 'clud', the Old English word for a small hill or collection of rock, or 'clod', a small lump of earth or clay. Roche Grange points to the French word *roche*, meaning rock, hence The Roaches. The Roaches itself is formed from Millstone Grit.

The area once belonged to the Cistercian monks of Dieulacres Abbey. The abbey was located just north of Leek and had extensive lands, including the Staffordshire moorlands. Like many other monastic operations in the area the main income was from wool. In the Middle Ages, large herds of sheep were reared for their wool, which was exported to Italy. One of the most famous customers for the monks of Dieulacres was the Black Prince (Prince Edward, the son of Edward III and heir to the throne, who died before his father). To maintain order and, no doubt, maintain income, the monks kept a band of men who would use strong-arm tactics and generally cause trouble for any person who did not toe the line; they even carried out incursions onto neighbouring lands for profit.

As you enter the centre of the hamlet take the first footpath on the left, across the front of a private house and out past a kennel, then through a steel gate to reach a farm track. Cross the track and head diagonally left across the field to a squeeze stile and gate in the left-hand hedge. Go through the gate and follow the wall NW through a steel field gate to begin the descent to a small stream. Walk around the hillside on your right to reach the footbridge and stile over the stream. Cross and bear right uphill, initially N, then NW, crossing a wire fence and arriving at **Buxton Brow**.

Go right, walking along the farm track then straight through the farmyard. Turn left at the top through the gate and walk up to the minor road. Turn right to **Clough Head**. As the road turns from tarmac to track ahead, take

The end of The Roaches looking onto Hen Cloud

the footpath on the right, passing through two gates as you cross the field to reach a minor road. Turn left and walk up the road and at the top, after crossing the cattle grid, turn right up the footpath onto **The Roaches** at **Roach End**.

Follow the footpath generally SE across the edge, passing the Ordnance Survey **triangulation pillar** and the **Doxey Pool**.

In the latter part of the 19th century, **The Roaches** formed part of the Swythanley Estate. The owner, Philip Brocklehurst, encouraged people to visit the edge to enjoy the fine views and natural history. He added Hen Cloud to the estate in later years.

The **Doxey Pool** is said to be inhabited by Jinny Greenteeth. According to the myth, if a mortal's eyes meet hers then they are doomed to be enticed into the depths of the pool, never to be seen again. The myth may have been a way of keeping children away from the waters. There is also a connection with the daughter of the woman who lived at Rockhall.

During the early part of the 20th century, Australian wallabies were released onto the Staffordshire moorlands where they survived for many years; some say they can still be seen in the 21st century, but no recent sighting has been confirmed.

To avoid a steep, rocky descent, take the footpath 300 metres SE of the Doxey Pool, that will lead back to the road and the lay-by. If you want to descend the end of The Roaches, carry on until the base of Hen Cloud is clearly in view and begin to descend by the rocky path, working your way to the left of the edge. Eventually you will reach a level path, with views across to Ramshaw Rocks. This path leads to the wall and access point for

The Doxey Pool

*Looking down the length of the Roaches to Hen
Cloud and beyond to the plains of central England*

Hen Cloud. Continue along this wall, bearing right to
visit Rockhall, or continuing straight on to return to the
road and the lay-by.

THE DON WHILLANS MEMORIAL HUT

The Don Whillans Memorial Hut is steeped in history. Its name is a poign-
ant commemoration of the first meeting of two of Britain's greatest climbers,
Don Whillan and Joe Brown. The two soon formed one of the great climbing
partnerships in the history of mountaineering.

The hut – actually a cave and cottage – was inhabited from the early
1800s, most recently by a couple until 1990. Originally intended as an
escape from the hustle and bustle of everyday life, the couple's tranquil existence was not to be, as the number of climbers and walkers increased almost
by the month. This at times brought uneasy tensions and often explosive
encounters. But the situation improved and a mutual respect was achieved
with the couple shouting advice to climbers, whether they wanted it or not.

WALK 22

Hollinsclough to Hollins Hill

Start/Finish	Hollinsclough SK 065 665
Distance	3.5 miles (6km)
Ascent/Descent	280m
Time	2hr
Terrain	Footpath, fields, road
Map	OS 1:25000 Explorer OL24
Refreshments	N/A
Parking	Hollinsclough SK 065 665

This walk is best savoured on a summer evening. Many will have the objective of reaching the top of Hollins Hill for the views of the Dragon's Back at sunset. But other treats are in store: the old packhorse bridge and ford crossing the River Dove below Tenterhill are a delightful surprise, as is the cobbled route as it climbs out of the valley.

Park outside the Methodist Chapel hall in **Hollinsclough**.

> The name **Hollinsclough** is thought to stem from the Old English for 'Howel's Ravine'. The population is much diminished nowadays, but once the place was thronged with hundreds of villagers. Silk weaving took place in the village, the finished product being transported over the hills via packhorse route to Macclesfield. The village is worth exploring for a few minutes. The old school and chapel are beautiful buildings. In summer the chapel hall serves tea and cakes to walkers.

Walk NW along the road out of the village and take the second footpath on the right by the Peak and Northern Footpaths Society notice pointing the way to Brand End and Brand Top via Washgate. Follow the footpath along

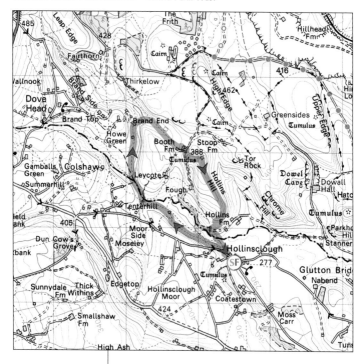

the hillside until it meets a wide grassy track bounded by old hawthorn trees. Turn right to follow the track downhill. After passing a barn on the left, keep following the fence on the right until you arrive at a small stone bridge over a stream. Cross this then turn left to go over a wooden stile and arrive at the beautiful packhorse bridge and paved route at Washgate, situated below **Tenterhill**.

> This old **packhorse route** over the River Dove was one of the ways the silk weavers transported goods to the mills in Macclesfield. The bridge is listed, and a recent traffic restriction order now protects the bridge, ford and route from further damage. Pay attention to the stone setts as you ascend the

track from the bridge; they give an idea of what the road surfaces were like in the days before tarmac and motorways. The bridge is an idyllically tranquil spot, beautiful for a moment's rest and in striking contrast to the throng of people on the same river in Dovedale.

Cross the bridge; you may ford the stream if the desire takes you. Then walk up the cobbled packhorse lane until you reach a footpath on the left by a bend. Go through the gate and follow the path along the hillside to eventually cross a small clapper bridge over the **River Dove**, then over a stile on the other side. Go up the banking, until the path forks, then take the right-hand fork up a steep slope until you reach the top of the hill S of **Howe Green**. Bear right along the hillside, crossing a stile after one field. After passing a small house on the left, join the farm track and go right to **Brand End**. Keep right, going between the farmhouse and buildings to follow the path down a walled lane via a metal gate.

The packhorse bridge over the River Dove at Washgate

Chrome Hill from Hollins Hill

If there is one hill in the Peak District that needs an Ordnance Survey triangulation pillar this is it.

If you do not want wet feet, retrace your steps through the gate to the signpost. Walk straight on, cross a wall and turn right to reach the stone bridge by the ford.

Cross a small clapper bridge then a stile and follow the footpath E, then SE, over a wooden stile to **Booth Farm**. At the farm go over the stone stile then bear diagonally left to cross a wooden stile. Turn right and walk through the gate onto the road. Go left, along the road, then right along the track heading into the fields. Follow the small signpost on the left up the steep hill. At the top, go through the gate on the left and follow the grassy track to the summit of **Hollins Hill**. ◄

Walk S from the summit to go through the gate and follow the concession path (not marked on the map) along the wall line SE down the ridge line of Hollins Hill. At the southern end, follow the path down through bushes to a wicket gate. Go left down the hill with the tumbled wall on your right until you reach a grassy track. Turn left and walk a few metres then follow the signpost right down a slope to a small signpost. Turn right here through trees to reach an open area of grass. Go left across the grass to a gate. Go through the gate and ford the stream. ◄

Once on the other side (using either ford or bridge) follow the footpath SE uphill, exiting onto a road via a gate. Go left and walk down the road into **Hollinsclough**.

WALK 23
Longnor to High Wheeldon

Start/Finish	Longnor SK 088 649
Distance	4.5 miles (7km)
Ascent/Descent	300m
Time	2.5hr
Terrain	Footpath, fields, road
Map	OS 1:25000 Explorer OL24
Refreshments	Longnor, Crowdicote
Parking	Longnor SK 088 649

Longnor is the jewel of this part of the SW White Peak. The village, once a thriving market town, has retained much of its charm, with cobbled alleyways and aged shopfronts giving it a Dickensian air. There are plenty of places to eat and drink in the village, making it a good base from which to explore the area. High Wheeldon is the perfect place for views at sunset and well worth the short ascent.

From the car park in the centre of **Longnor** walk E along High Street. After passing Ye Olde Cheshire Cheese pub on your left, take the footpath next right, opposite the imposing pair of townhouses. Walk down to the farm and bear left across the yard and exit via a steel gate. Go diagonally right to pass through a wicket gate then follow the wall on your left, crossing six fields through gate or squeeze stile to arrive in front of a farmhouse. Turn right to exit the small enclosure by a steel gate, then head SE across fields. Just after you cross a brook, follow a wall to a corner and turn left, then take the squeeze stile and gate combination to the left of the field gate.

Walk straight ahead, aiming for the right of the house in front of you, and pass through the wicket gate to ascend the field, keeping to the right. Pass through a second gate to exit via a gate onto the road at **Edgetop**. Go

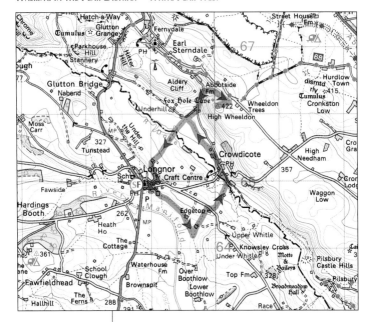

Crowdicote (Cruda's Cot) sits on a packhorse route that worked its way from Leek to Bakewell; the bridge across the River Dove provided a major crossing.

right, crossing the road to take the footpath down through trees, then out through a gate into a field. Head NE to the bottom of the field and cross the footbridge over the **River Dove**. Walk up the track and turn left to walk to the road, then turn right up to **Crowdicote**. ◄

Opposite the Packhorse Inn, take the minor road on the left, just before the bend and, after passing a row of cottages, go left down a lane and follow this NW past Meadow Farm. Then walk across fields to enter Green Lane via a stone stile. Go right to the road and continue NE until you reach the quarry below **Aldery Cliff** ◄ After visiting the quarry, cross the road and go over the stile to follow the grassy path up to the top of **High Wheeldon**.

The quarry is worth visiting for its wealth of wildflowers. Pay attention to the notice from the British Mountaineering Club.

High Wheeldon, **Parkhouse Hill** and **Chrome Hill** are the remnants of limestone apron reefs that were created when the area sat on the equator many

136

millions of years ago. Fox Hole Cave, below the summit of High Wheeldon, is now gated. Remains found in the cave would suggest it has been in use since the Neolithic period. At sunset, the hill is a perfect vantage point from which to view the Dove and Manifold valleys, with the sun setting over the Dragon's Back (Chrome Hill).

Retrace your steps to Aldery Cliff and follow the road down to enter Green Lane once again. This time continue SW along the lane, crossing Beggar's Bridge, a footbridge over the **River Dove**, then ascending the hill and aiming for the right of the barn in the bottom of the next valley. Follow the footpath around the back of the barn and walk up the farm track, passing through two gates to exit onto a road. Go left, then take the next road on the right, through Top o' th' Edge, and follow the road downhill until you arrive back on High Street, turning right to return to the centre of **Longnor**.

The limestone reef of Parkhouse Hill and Chrome Hill from High Wheeldon

WALK 24
Hen Cloud

Start/Finish	Upper Hulme SK 013 609
Distance	4.5 miles (7.5km)
Ascent/Descent	335m
Time	2.5hr
Terrain	Footpath, moorland, road
Map	OS 1:25000 Explorer OL24
Refreshments	Upper Hulme
Parking	On-street parking, Upper Hulme

This is a lovely morning or afternoon walk, to be enjoyed before sampling the delights of Upper Hulme. The walk can be combined with The Roaches (Walk 21) to make a full day out. The focal point of the walk is the escarpments of Ramshaw Rocks and Hen Cloud. Here we step from the limestone country of pasture and farm, into gritstone country of sparsely populated high moorland, giving spectacular views across the lowlands of the south.

From Ye Olde Rock Inn in **Upper Hulme**, walk SW downhill then turn right at the first junction, continuing down to the bridge and ford in the heart of the tiny hamlet. Turn right by the ford and walk uphill between houses along a concrete road, maintaining the course until you arrive at Dains Mill. Go to the left of the mill and pass through a gate, then bear immediately right. A little further on, go through two smaller gates, following the stream on your right, to a small wicket gate leading into open country. Bear left of the ruined barn ahead, up a short bank to go through a gate. Turn right along the wall line on your right, cross a small stream and take the wooden stile into private property. Keep to the public right of way and turn right along the driveway that runs to the house.

Go through a gate and across the farm track at **Naychurch**. Turn left along the public right of way leading directly through the farmyard. Cross the cattle grid and continue straight ahead along the farm track to the junction with the **A53**. Turn left before the road, following the waymarked sign across heather moorland, then cross the minor road and ascend the short steep section onto **Ramshaw Rocks**.

The rough sandstone of **Ramshaw Rocks** was formed around 320 million years ago. The purplish tinge indicates it is Roaches grit, the rock getting its name from the nearby Roaches. If you travelled from Buxton along the A53 you will have passed a pub on the left call the Winking Man. It takes its name from a hole through the rock on Ramshaw

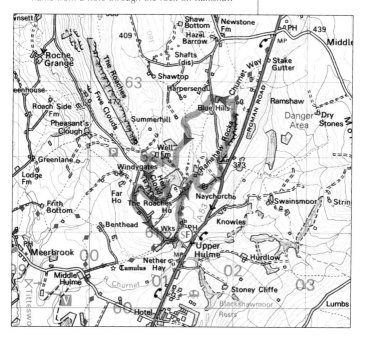

Rocks, that seems to wink as people travel past. The area is rich in fauna and flora: curlew, kestrel, merlin and buzzard are frequently seen along the escarpment and moorland and billberry and the Killarney fern are present too.

Continue walking along the escarpment, generally N, until you come to a drystone-walled enclosure. Go through the gate and head N along the line of the wall on your right, exiting via a gate, then follow the wall left down across the moor to the road. Go left and take the footpath almost immediately on the right, where the sign for Misty Hill is, then go SW across **Blue Hills** and follow the wall line down, ignoring the first path on the left and taking the gate that leads across a small field to a second

Climbers on Hen Cloud

gate. Go through this and bear left, to drop down into a small valley E of **Summerhill**.

Cross the stream and go through the gate opposite to ascend the small hill, then follow the fence line SE then S, eventually passing through two gates to exit onto the farm track leading to **Well Farm**. Turn right and, just before entering the farmyard, go left, following the footpath sign across a narrow field, exiting via a stile to cross a stream and walk up the bank opposite. When you arrive at a footpath sign, no more than 50 metres from the stream, go right and follow the path NW to the wall that separates Hen Cloud from The Roaches. At the gate in the wall turn left and walk up to the top of **Hen Cloud**. ▸

If you wish to continue on to The Roaches walk (Walk 21), go right, through the gate and the next gate ahead to ascend to the gritstone edge.

> **Hen Cloud**, meaning 'Hen Hill' in Norse, is a wonderful place to sit and admire the views across the flat planes of Staffordshire to the mountains of Wales – Snowdonia being easily visible on a clear day. After an absence of many years, peregrines have returned to nest on Hen Cloud and have begun to breed. As a result, the face of Hen Cloud is closed to climbers for the breeding season.

Follow the escarpment S then turn NE until the path meets with another by a disused quarry. Take this path S down to **Roaches House**, passing through the wooden gate onto the private drive. Follow the drive out of the grounds below Hen Cloud, exiting onto the road. Turn left and follow the road back into the centre of **Upper Hulme**. At the ford bear right, walking up the hill to the road junction. Turn left, continuing the climb until you reach the pub again, which will by now be open and a welcome sight.

WALK 25

Upper Hulme to Blake Mere

Start/Finish	Upper Hulme SK 013 609
Distance	5.5 miles (8.5km)
Ascent/Descent	375m
Time	3hr
Terrain	Footpath, fields, road
Map	OS 1:25000 Explorer OL24
Refreshments	Ye Olde Rock Inn, Upper Hulme
Parking	Upper Hulme SK 013 609

This route introduces you to the wilder moorland terrain of the South-West Peak District. The walk begins in Upper Hulme a village that was centred around the silk trade. It then heads over moorland to Merryton Low and Blake Mere, giving excellent views along the way of the gritstone edges of Hen Cloud, Ramshaw Rock and The Roaches, before descending via a beautiful bridleway back to the village.

From the Ye Olde Rock Inn in **Upper Hulme**, walk SW down the road and at the junction go sharp right down into the village centre. Follow the road past the ford and ascend past the old silk factory. After the road sweeps right, look for the next junction, hidden by a house on the left.

There has been a silk mill at **Upper Hulme** for several hundred years. Dieulacres Abbey had a mill in production in the 13th century. By the 19th century silk throwsters, men who twisted silk yarn before winding it onto a bobbin, lived in cottages in the village. By the latter part of the 19th century the mill was used for dyeing by Leek silk manufacturer William Tatton. Production continued until 1970, when it was moved to Leek.

Turn left here and go over the stile by the telegraph poles, then follow the footpath across fields, descending through trees to exit onto the **A53**. Cross the road bearing right and take the lane on the left up to the farm at **Hurdlow**. Go straight on through the farmyard and gate, keeping to the wide track. After passing through a kissing gate follow the track right, then leave it at the signpost that is pointing SE to Mermaid and Morridge. Follow the yellow marker posts E across the moor, stepping over two stone stiles, eventually arriving at The Mermaid a former public house.

Cross the road to the junction ahead of you, then go NE over open moorland to arrive at **Merryton Low triangulation pillar** and barrow. Go N from the trig to the road junction and cross to Blake Mere on the left.

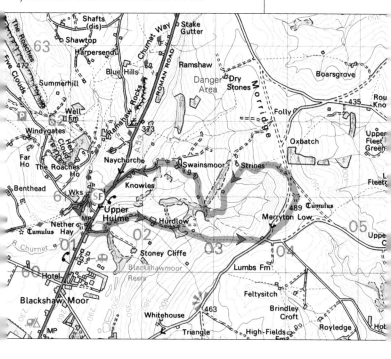

THE MERMAID PUB

The Mermaid sits on what was the Great Drove Road that was used to transport livestock from west to east across the middle of England. The pub got its name from the legend of Blake Mere, sometimes called the Mermaid Pond. Local legend tells of a young woman who was tried as a witch for refusing the advances of a local man. It is said she was drowned in the pool but, shortly before her death, placed a curse on the man who was found dead by the pond three days later. The pond was said to be bottomless and, during the 19th century, locals attempted to drain it; the channel they dug is still in evidence. As they worked, a mermaid appeared and told them that, if they continued, she would drown the inhabitants of Leek. So, they stopped. In the middle of the 20th century local divers explored the pool and found it to be no more than six feet deep and full of mud.

Scout in the cotton grass on Merryton Low

From Blake Mere take the track generally W to a stile where you access farm pasture. Follow the natural ridge line SW to the remains of a building then go directly S, following a sheep trod down by the edge of woodland to meet a stream. Bear right and cross the stream at a suitable point then ascend the opposite bank, using the sheep trod as a guide until you join with the grassy sward of the bridleway. Go right and follow the green track downhill, crossing a ford at the bottom and rising up the opposite side via a gate and low wall that sweeps left into open fields.

Head NW, aiming to the right of the barn on the horizon, then continue on through three gates to the farm at **Swainsmoor**. Follow the track through the farm and out of the gate to a larger farm ahead, with Ramshaw Rocks towering in the distance behind. Walk between the farm buildings and, just as you exit, go left to a wall and follow this right, all the way down to the farm track and gate. Go through the gate to the left to avoid the cattle grid and follow the track sweeping right, uphill, passing by the settlement of **Knowles** on the left until you reach the **A53**. Turn left along the grass verge, then cross the road when the junction for **Upper Hulme** appears and return to the public house.

Ramshaw Rocks from the ancient track at Swainsmoor

WALK 26
Upper Elkstone to Lumbs Farm

Start/Finish	Upper Elkstone SK 055 590
Distance	6 miles (9.5km)
Ascent/Descent	380m
Time	3hr
Terrain	Footpath, fields, and road
Map	OS 1:25000 Explorer OL24
Refreshments	None
Parking	Street parking, Upper Elkstone SK 055 590

This walk from Upper Elkstone passes Herbage Barn – a lonely sight today, but once on a major packhorse route – the remains of which can be seen on the northern side of the road. The Ordnance Survey triangulation pillar at Under the Hill offers superb panoramic views. Parking is limited. Please be considerate of residents. For a longer day, the walk can be combined with Walk 28, Onecote to Old Mixon Hay.

From the centre of **Upper Elkstone**, walk up the drive to the Manor Farm. Go through the gate at the right of the manor house, following the waymark signs that lead you between the two barns to enter a field via a metal gate. Walk down the field and, after passing through another gate, head diagonally right and cross the brook at the bottom via the footbridge. Go left, working your way up to farm buildings. Herbage Barn will become evident on your right as you ascend the hillside. Follow the track through Herbage until just after it turns sharp right. Head NE across the moor aiming for the left of Herbage Barn. Go over the stile and across the road, then through a gate.

Follow the public footpath NE a short distance to go through a gate and follow the field boundary around **Upper Hey Corner**, turning almost N to cross a small stream. Continue making your way down the hillside

THE GREAT DROVE ROAD

The deep scars you see in front of you as you go through the gate are the remains of the Great Drove Road that ran from Cheshire across the Peak to Nottinghamshire. Herbage Barn and the surrounding pasture provided a perfect place to stop. The drovers transported huge herds of cattle and needed places where they could stop overnight and hold the livestock safely. Before the cattle made the journey, their hoofs would be shod. This would add to the destruction of the ground, evidence of which can still be seen today. As well as cattle, the drovers transported vast flocks of geese and turkey along the Great Drove Road on their way to market. Before the journey began the birds would be driven through tar and then sand to protect their feet against the arduous terrain.

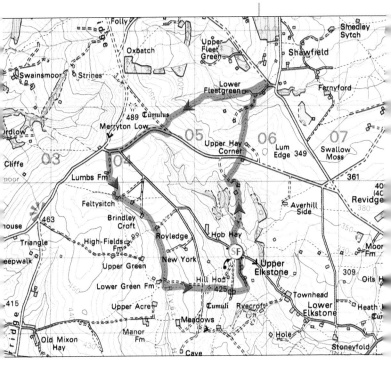

until you come to a shallow ford. Cross the stream and go through the gate, turning right along the track. At the next track junction go right then, at the road, turn left a few metres and take the footpath SW across several stiles to the farm at **Lower Fleetgreen**. Bear left then right through the farmyard and exit via the gate in the wall corner beneath powerlines.

Follow the footpath across a footbridge and then a ladder stile to reach a second footbridge over a steep-sided stream. Cross and bear left, working your way up the hillside. As you walk up the gentle hill keep to the right of the building ruins then follow the remains of a wall and ditch to reach a stile leading onto open access land. Follow the faint path SW, passing a permanent Orienteering marker post until you exit onto a minor road. Go left to reach the junction of the road leading to Herbage Barn.

Bear right along the road towards Leek until you arrive at the farm track to **Lumbs Farm**. Walk down the track, carrying straight on past the farm buildings and go over the stile into a field. Go left following the field boundary around the field to a gain a farm track at **Feltysitch**.

Go left then immediately right up a slight hill to a stile in a stone wall. Go over the stile and head for the house straight ahead, entering the garden by the gate then bearing left and right along the drive. Turn right by the hedge and follow the footpath around the perimeter of the field to a stile. Go over the stile and cross the track, then follow the footpath SE across fields and stiles past **Brindley Croft**. Maintain the same course to **Royledge**. Keep to the right of the house and bear right along the track through the wooden gate. Walk S across the fields, using stiles to arrive at the ford below **Lower Green Farm**.

If you wish to carry on to the walk taking in Onecote to Old Mixon Hay (Walk 28), go straight on, following the footpath S to the footbridge over the River Hamps. Cross this and go up the hillside towards Manor Farm, then bear left to reach the gate and join the directions for the walk.

If keeping to this walk, go left at the ford and follow the old packhorse route uphill, initially in a holloway, then a farm track, then cross a short stretch of field via gate and stile to reach the road. Cross the road and go over the stile to arrive at the **triangulation pillar** at Under the Hill. Continue E down the hillside through two small gates to exit onto a farm track. Go left, then immediately right over a stile and walk downhill until you meet a wide farm track by the corner of a hedgerow. Turn left along the track to return to **Upper Elkstone**.

The view across the valley shows the old road to Cheadle going through Lower Green Farm

WALK 27
Leek to Gun

Start/Finish	Leek SJ 984 565
Distance	14.5 miles (23.5km)
Ascent/Descent	420m
Time	7hr
Terrain	Footpath, fields, road
Map	OS 1:25000 Explorer OL24
Refreshments	Leek, Tittesworth, Rushton Spencer, Rudyard
Parking	On-street parking or car parks in Leek

This is a long, but surprisingly relaxing walk from the market town of Leek to the vantage point of Gun, a hill with stunning views across the White Peak, the Cheshire Plain with Jodrell Bank, down into Wales and the hills of the Long Mynd. On the way the walk passes along the shores of Tittesworth and Rudyard reservoirs, one offering a wealth of bird life while the other offers trains and waterside homes.

From the Buttercross in **Leek** market square, walk N and turn right, along the **A53**, Stockwell Street. Turn left at the crossroad, heading for Ball Haye Green Industrial Estate, following the Ball Haye Road as it sweeps right and heads NE. Just after the recreation ground on the left, turn left into Tittesworth Avenue and follow this around until the next junction on the left. Turn left into Nightingale Gardens then take the public footpath on the right. Proceed along the path until you have passed through two kissing gates to exit onto a road. Turn left then take the footpath, first right, down across a footbridge spanning a stream, ascending steps into open grass land.

Walk uphill, continuing through a gate until you reach level ground by a bench seat. Turn left by the fence, walking across duckboards and through a gate to proceed generally N across fields and through a kissing gate to reach woodland and a fingerpost. Go right, following the markers for the Long Trail to the visitor centre at **Tittesworth Reservoir**. On reaching the visitor car park bear right to leave it behind, following the exit to the main road. Turn left at the junction and cross over the road as you walk across the bridge. Turn right at the next junction to reach the village of **Meerbrook**.

After passing The Lazy Trout public house, go right at the junction and walk along the road for 500 metres, then take the footpath on the left across fields heading NW until you reach a farm track. Turn left, continuing W where the paths cross, to take the farm track past solar panels and into the farmyard at Lower Wetwood. Go straight ahead between the buildings, bearing right in front of the large barn, passing through a gate to follow the concrete track down to a fingerpost pointing the way to Oldhay Top. Turn left and follow the footpath behind the large barn then go over the stile, straight ahead by the metal gate.

Bear right up the slope and, following the fingerpost, cross the stream hidden in the hedge. Go NW up the field towards **Oldhay Top**. Exit via a stone stile and walk straight on uphill over a wooden stile to join a concrete track. Follow the track uphill and, on reaching the top, turn left along the drive to New Zealand. Just before entering the private grounds, bear right along the footpath at the rear of the property to take the access stile over the fence and ascend to the Ordnance Survey **triangulation pillar** on **Gun**.

GUN

Gun is a wonderful place to stop and have lunch. The views from the top are magnificent. The white dish of Jodrell Bank can clearly be seen on the Cheshire Plain. Bosley Cloud, a prominent hill to the north-west, is also the site of a 'double sunset', where the sun seemingly sets then rises again before reaching its final resting place. To the east there are superb views of Hen Cloud, The Roaches and Ramshaw Rocks. On a clear day it is possible to see Wales and the Brecon Beacons as well as Long Mynd. In the north is the magnificent view of Shutlingsloe, looking like a giant wave about to break. Gun is generally quiet, the throngs having been drawn to the gritstone of The Roaches, so you may well have the place to yourself.

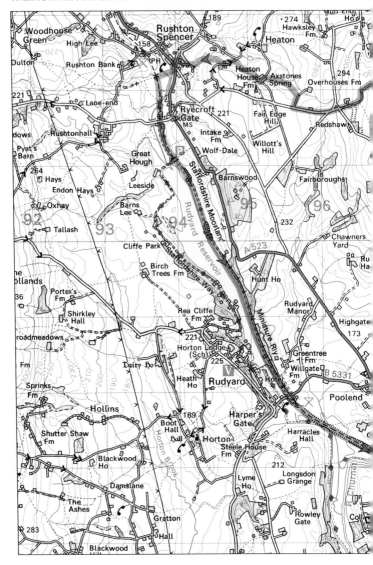

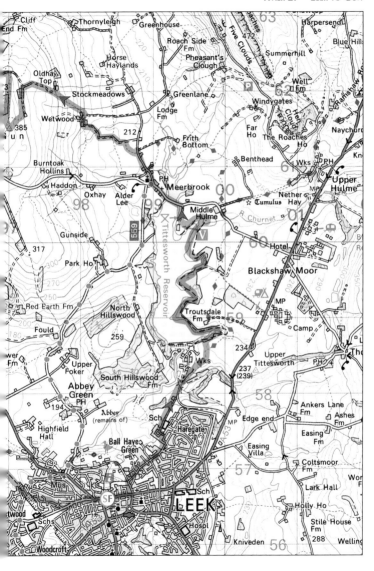

Hen Cloud (Hen Hill) from Gun

From the trig pillar, walk directly N towards Shutlingsloe along the well-defined track, passing the menhir – standing stone – and exiting onto a minor road via a gate. Turn left along the concrete track and follow this downhill until it joins a minor road. At the junction go straight across, passing the woodland on your right. At the next junction go straight across again, heading W along the road to the driveway to **Overhouses Farm**. Turn right down the drive and, after passing over the cattle grid, go immediately left through the gate and follow the footpath NW, then W to reach a minor road. Go over the stile by a spring decanting into a stone water trough at **Axestones Spring**. Turn left and walk to the corner, then take the footpath on the right along the left-hand side of the stone wall.

At the wall corner, continue straight ahead to a stile leading onto a minor road. Go left along the road and, just after passing a detached house on the right, go through the squeeze stile to the right into fields. Bear left following the boundary of the tree plantation, over one wooden stile and, a little further on, a wooden gate at the corner of the hedge. Turn right following the hedge down to a farm gate. Go through the gate and proceed straight on, down the tarmac lane to the junction with a minor road at **Rushton Spencer**. Turn left, then at the next junction turn right, in front of The Royal Oak, and cross the road. Take the next footpath on the left into fields, following around to the right to go over a small footbridge. Continue to the hedge line ahead and ascend the slope to a stone bridge. Go left over a stile just before the bridge and join the wide trail, heading left to **Rudyard Reservoir**, passing the Rudyard steam railway station along the way.

> **Rudyard Reservoir** was constructed in the late 18th century to feed the Caldon Canal. Sometime later, its proximity to the newly created rail networks brought visitors to the water, giving rise to a vibrant

The railway by Rudyard Reservoir

155

tourist attraction. Today there is sailing, fishing, walking and cycling in or around the area. There's a visitor centre and tearoom near the dam.

Continue along the trail as you pass the dam. After crossing the bridges over the **River Churnet**, the trail nears its end. Bear left as the trail heads up a slope to reach a road; do not follow the faint footpath into the cutting, the way is blocked. Continue to the housing estate road to the end of Westview Close on the outskirts of Leek. At the junction go straight ahead onto a footpath between houses, following this in a SE direction until you arrive at the junction with Westwood Road. Turn left and follow the road back into the centre of **Leek**.

A Leek building saved by William Morris

WALK 28

Onecote to Old Mixon Hay

Start/Finish	Onecote SK 049 551
Distance	6 miles (9.5km)
Ascent/Descent	235m
Time	3hr
Terrain	Footpath, fields, and road
Map	OS 1:25000 Explorer OL24
Refreshments	Onecote
Parking	Onecote village hall SK 049 551

This route through a lived-in landscape with deep, historical connections can be combined with Walk 26, Upper Elkstone to Lumbs Farm, to complete a full day's walk. Onecote village has a history of farming, sheep rearing and mining. The Jervis Arms is a traditional country pub that makes for a fulfilling end to a day of walking.

From the village hall in **Onecote** walk NW past the church and take the first road right to **Onecote Grange Farm**. Bear left at the fork and then follow the track around the barn on the right. Aim for the top left-hand corner of the field on the left, go through the gate then follow the wall line NW. After 150 metres cross over the wall and continue in the same direction, following the power lines and crossing four stiles and a footbridge. At the corner of a fence on the right, go left and skirt around the bushes in front of you to find the fingerpost pointing the way to the footbridge across a stream.

Go past the farm at **Waterhouse** crossing the access lane and subsequent field to enter, via a stile, a narrow pasture close to the stream on the left. Follow the path through the pasture, leaving by a stile onto more open land. Keep on the path, now going N, until you meet the track to **Newhouse Farm**. Go left, and at the ford,

*Cottage in Onecote
dated 1677*

cross the small footbridge to the right to gain access to the stile. Go over the stile and up the bank to a farm track. Take the track uphill then follow the waymarked signs to the right, down towards the stream. Track the water upstream until you reach the tarmac lane leading to **New Mixon**.

> The land around this area was known as the Wastes, formerly common lands before they were enclosed. The name **Mixon** comes from the medieval word for 'midden', or 'dung hill'.

Cross the track and follow the footpath through the farmyard at **Old Mixon Hay**, leaving the farm by the gates onto a wide lane. Go right, to ascend then descend the ridge, and drop down by the access lane to **Manor Farm**. Go through a gate after the cattle grid towards the **River Hamps**.

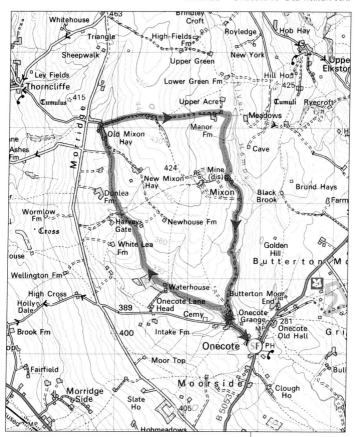

If you wish to carry on to Walk 26, Upper Elkstone to Lumbs Farm, go straight on down the field and cross the River Hamps by the footbridge. Turn left and follow the footpath N to the ford below Lower Green Farm, where the eastern path to Upper Elkstone is met.

To continue with this walk, after going through the gate, turn right to a farm gate in the wall. After passing through the gate, continue along the course of the

Wildflowers by one of the many fords in the White Peak

Mixon Mine has deposits of lead and copper and was mined in several periods over the last few centuries.

Hamps Way, crossing several fields, generally S, until you reach a farm track. Follow the waymark post uphill and along the front of the barn. Cross the stile and then go through the narrow squeeze stile in the wall to arrive at **Mixon Mine**. ◄

Go straight ahead down the track, keeping the abandoned farmhouse on the right. Go over the stile and turn right along the tarmac lane, following this all the way until it splits just before **Onecote Grange Farm**. Take the left-hand fork and walk down, through the farmyard gate and out via the white gate at the bottom. Turn left, then left again at the junction to return to **Onecote** village hall.

WALK 29

Hulme End to Revidge

Start/Finish	Hulme End SK 103 593
Distance	6 miles (9.5km)
Ascent/Descent	230m
Time	3hr
Terrain	Footpath, fields and moorland
Map	OS 1:25000 Explorer OL24
Refreshments	Hulme End, Warslow
Parking	Hulme End SK 103 593

The walk starts at Hulme End, a hamlet that was at the northern end of the Leek and Manifold Valley Light Railway. This line carried milk and tourists. It now forms the 8-mile (13-km) foot and cycle trail, Manifold Way. This walk begins along the track then follows a gentle ascent passing through the village of Warslow to the moorland summit of Revidge, with its excellent views of the surrounding countryside.

From **Hulme End** follow the signpost for the Manifold Track until you reach a gate and, beyond, a road. Go through the gate and cross the road to continue along the Manifold Track. Walk over two bridges and pass by **Ecton** limestone bed geological feature, sloping upwards on your right, until you come to a gate across the track. Go through and, after a few metres, turn right up a slope then step over a stile and turn right again to follow the fence line out of the trees and over a stile into open pasture. Follow the footpath NW across several fields and squeeze stiles always keeping the small brook to your right. When you reach the minor road by Ivy House Farm, turn right and walk to the main road running through **Warslow**. Turn right along the road through the village, the B5053. Cross the road at the junction to continue NW along Leek Road, towards The Greyhound Inn. ▶

If the inn is closed and you are in need of refreshment, there are springs around the village where drinking water, once bottled and sold, can now be obtained freely.

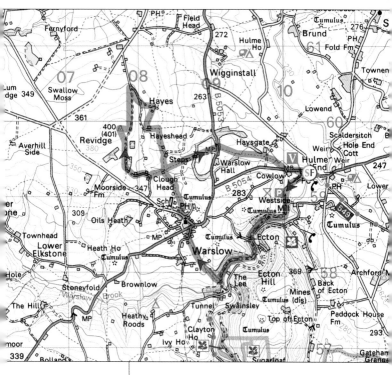

After passing the inn, go right at the next junction and follow the signposted public footpath behind the inn. Bear left to reach a squeeze stile and gate. Go through and continue in the same direction, keeping the school boundary on your left. After passing through four stiles or gates you arrive at a signpost. Follow the finger left to reach a gate in a wall, go through and across the field keeping to the left of the derelict barn, then go W to a stile leading into a walled lane. Walk along the lane a few metres then turn right along a farm track to **Clough Head**.

Proceed straight past the farmhouse on your right and enter a field through a small gate and follow the sunken footpath up to the left of a barn. Go over a stile

and follow the wall on your right to the far corner of a plantation. Go through the squeeze stile in the wall on the right and follow the edge of the trees to exit via a gate onto moorland at **Revidge**. Follow the tree line until you come to a footpath taking you to the Ordnance Survey **triangulation pillar**.

The view north from Revidge towards Buxton

> The **views from the triangulation pillar** are spectacular. In the north you can see the Dragon's Back (Chrome Hill), Parkhouse Hill and, in the far distance, Axe Edge. To the west is Merryton Low. To the east is Ecton Mine. And to the south is Thors Cave.

Retrace your steps to the trees and head directly N to meet a farm track.

Note the Ministry of Defence sign. To find details of exercises, check the website: www.gov.uk/government/publications/leek-and-upper-hulme-firing-times. ▶

Never pick anything up in this area.

Turn right along the track and follow it down to the farm at **Hayes**. As you enter the yard turn right to follow the walled lane out onto open fields. Keep following the wall on the left to go through the gate by the abandoned farmhouse at **Hayeshead**. Opposite the building, take the footpath signposted right across a field then through two gates at the side of Hayes Cottage. Follow the fence to descend a short flight of steps and cross a stream to the corner of a cottage at **Steps**. Continue S along the rear of the cottage until you reach a gate and squeeze stile that lead to a concrete bridge. Go through the gate but do not cross the bridge. Turn left across the field and through a further two gates then along another field to pass behind the farm buildings at Upper Brownhill and exit via a gate. Bear left, following the power lines to the NE corner of the field. Go over the stile hidden in the hedge, taking care as it leads directly onto the **B5053**.

WARSLOW HALL

Warslow Hall and the surrounding land was the summer residence of the Harpur Crewe family who lived the rest of the year at Calke Abbey in the south of Derbyshire. The heirs to the Harpur Crewe baronetcy had a reputation for being eccentric and the 10th and last baronet was no exception. A keen outdoorsman he amassed a collection of several thousand stuffed birds. He preferred the loneliness of the woodlands to the company of people. He would issue notices to tenants not to carry out hedging so that birds would have a greater choice of nesting site, a view that was almost a hundred years ahead of its time. His relationship with his children, however, was more troublesome. He communicated with them by letter, preferring not to have any form of personal communication. He died in 1924, the last of the line.

Cross the road and go over the stile to the right of the metal farm gate and bear diagonally right across the field to a gate. Go through and follow the fence line on your left to eventually cross a farm track leading to **Haysgate**. Cross the track and bear right, following the stream on your left until you reach a stile leading onto the **B5054**. Go left along the road to return to the car park at **Hulme End**.

WALK 30

Grindon to Butterton

Start/Finish	Grindon SK 084 545
Distance	7 miles (11km)
Ascent/Descent	285m
Time	3.5hr
Terrain	Footpath, fields, road
Map	OS 1:25000 Explorer OL24
Refreshments	Butterton
Parking	Grindon SK 084 545

This walk offers two wonderful churches, a country pub and a village street that runs through a ford. Along with that, you'll see some wonderful countryside and the remnants of a medieval field system. The gargoyles at Grindon are a delight, while Butterton basks in its picture-postcard ford. Take time on the walk and absorb and enjoy what this part of the countryside has to offer.

▶ Walk W away from the church tower at **Grindon** and go through the left of the two gates ahead of you. Follow the fingerpost and the sign for the Cairn to 47 Squadron. The path goes through a series of stiles and gates as it works its way first W, then NW, across fields to reach the minor road at **Grindonmoor Gate** via a stone stile. Cross the road and go through the gap in the wall opposite, then bear right to the corner of the small enclosure, exiting by the stile.

Walk straight ahead between the low building and the telegraph pole, keeping to the left of the oil tank, to follow the fingerpost direction NW across a field. Cross a fence and then, as you approach a wide metal gate in front of a tall pole supporting power lines, go left down the field. Cross a stile and then go through a farm gate to join a wide track. Follow the track SW until the footpath

Before leaving the car park by Grindon Church, examine the gargoyles and carvings of humans and animals that play around the church tower and doorway.

leaves it at the entrance to a farmyard. Take the diversion going right, across a field. Go through the wicket gate, then left down the field, emerging onto a drive by a wooden building that leads you onto the road at **Ford**.

Go right, along the road. As you come to the bridge over the **River Hamps**, go right, then left, following the fingerpost down a driveway to the right of a cattle grid. Continue along the footpath as it passes out of the property by a wicket gate, and proceeds along a well-made farm track forming part of the Hamps Way. As the track sweeps right up to **Bullclough**, continue NW over the stile to the left of a farm gate. Follow the trail over the flood plain, crossing a footbridge and a stone wall, then finally a wooden stile that delivers you onto the **B5053** at **Onecote**.

Walk right, up the road, and take the first road junction on the right, uphill until it sweeps sharp right, then go straight ahead, across the stile. Walk up the moor, aiming for the right of the derelict barn in the trees on the horizon. Enter **Grindon Moor**, bearing right at the National Trust sign, cross a stile and continue NE across the moor, leaving it by a gate onto a minor road.

WINTER ON GRINDON MOOR

On 23 January 1947 snow started to fall across Britain. It continued to fall somewhere in the country for 55 days. Temperatures dropped to -21°C and the wind caused the snow to drift several metres deep in places. High ground, particularly the Pennines, were badly affected, effectively cutting off the people from the surrounding communities. Things became desperate, with many isolated villages and hamlets running out of food. The RAF were tasked with dropping food supplies and one of the landing zones was around Butterton. On the 13 February, the crew of an RAF Halifax set out to drop supplies at a site near Butterton. Low cloud and poor visibility shrouded the site and at some point, after the first attempt, the plane hit the top of Grindon Moor.

When members from RAF Mountain Rescue at Harpur Hill reached the crashed aircraft, they found that villagers had already removed the bodies of all eight occupants who had perished in the crash. A memorial was erected close to the crash site on Grindon Moor at SK 063 553.

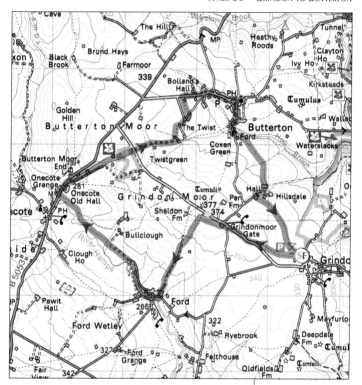

Cross the road and go through the gate straight ahead, then down a farm track that crosses **Butterton Moor**. Follow the waymarks past **Twistgreen** to a narrow field bordered by hedges. Just before you reach a long, derelict farm building on the right, go left towards the small stone barn. Walk behind the barn and cross the footbridge across the stream, then ascend the hillside to join a farm track. Walk along the track, keeping left at the farm. After passing through a metal gate, go immediately left over the stile and follow the wall line, generally N, crossing a footbridge, then a stile to reach the road into **Butterton**. Go right and walk down into Butterton village.

The ford at Butterton

Butterton takes its name from the pastures and hills that surround it; the pasture provided good grazing and gave excellent butter. A wake takes place every August bank holiday to celebrate the birth of St Bartholemew, who the church is dedicated to. The village is one of only two Doubly Thankful villages in the White Peak (the other being Bradbourne), where all residents who took part in both world wars returned safely.

Follow the road to the church then descend past the Black Lion Inn on your right and through the cobbled ford at the bottom. Ascend the other side until you reach the first public footpath on the left. Follow the public footpath along the concrete track then out onto open fields. ◄

Note the narrow strip fields on the hillside opposite.

Walk SE along the footpath, crossing two stiles then going over a small stream and through a gate to ascend the hillside to **Hillsdale Hall**. Follow the footpath through the farm and out onto a minor road. Go right, up the road, and at the farm entrance on the left, enter the farmyard, turning immediately left, then straight ahead to leave by a steel gate located between two buildings. Walk down the field, cross a stile, then bear SE, using the combination of two stiles and a footbridge to cross a ditch. Follow the hedge line on your right through four squeeze stiles then finally exit the fields through the gate and into the car park at **Grindon**.

WALK 31

Hartington to Sheen

Start/Finish	Hartington SK 128 604
Distance	7 miles (11km)
Ascent/Descent	265m
Time	3hr
Terrain	Footpath, fields, road
Map	OS 1:25000 Explorer OL24
Refreshments	Hartington
Parking	Hartington SK 128 604

This walk highlights some of the beautiful landscape and communities of the White Peak. It is a gentle walk through a landscape that has little changed in centuries. The hamlet of Brund is a surprise, the few houses of golden stone settled around the courtyard. Sheen is interesting too. The church seems out of place, until one realises that a landlord wanted to make this village the 'Athens of Derbyshire'.

From the front of the Charles Cotton Hotel in **Hartington** walk towards the duck pond then turn W along Stonewell Lane until you reach a new housing development. Turn right through the gate following the Peak and Northern Footpaths sign to Sheen. Follow the path to the left of the power lines through a wooded copse. Coming out of the trees, go NW using stiles and gates across fields to a small metal bridge and your first encounter with the **River Dove**. Cross the bridge and continue in the same direction to exit the field into a fenced lane leading to **Bridge-end**.

Bear diagonally left, taking the public footpath uphill aiming for the top corner of the wall ahead. Go over the stile and follow the wall on the right to cross a second stile, then walk diagonally left across the field to the nearest corner of the house at Crakelow. Go over a stile and walk W down the field to a footbridge crossing a stream.

Cross the bridge and walk up the hillside veering right around the wall corner to keep to the right of the farm at Newfield and reach a gate. Go through the gate and bear left across a field to exit via a gate onto the road. Go right up the road towards **Townend**. Walk straight ahead at the crossroad following the road downhill until you meet a signposted footpath on the left as the road swings right.

Follow the fingerpost down the walled lane, through two steel farm gates, keeping the wall on your right as it turns NW towards Brund. Just after you pass a stone barn, walk down to a stream, crossing it then keeping on the same direction to meet a road. Go through the stile and follow the road into **Brund**. ▶

Walk past the hamlet then take the first footpath on the left across fields to meet the road again lower down. Turn right, to the road junction, then left, and take the footpath on the left through a narrow opening between fence and wall. At the end of the path turn right and follow the fingerpost for Longnor, joining the Manifold Trail. Go through a gate into woodland, leaving the trees by a second gate. Then descend to the valley floor and follow the trail heading upstream of the **River Manifold**. After passing through wet pasture, the footpath begins to rise, crossing a series of stone walls via stiles to reach a gate. Go through and walk straight ahead to a second gate, then walk to the left of a house and follow the fingerpost pointing the way through a gate to cross a stream at **Pool**.

After the stream, the path goes almost due N, crossing a walled lane and maintaining course to pass by a large barn on your left. Shortly after the barn, cross a footbridge and head for the left of the farm ahead at **Lower Boothlow**. Follow the footpath almost E around the farm to join the wide track that dips and curves its way up to a minor road. Turn right along the road then take the first footpath on the left, heading SE across fields to a wooden footbridge over a stream. Cross and go right up the bank, over the stile then bear left along the wall line towards the house straight ahead at **Hill End**. Keep to the right of the house following the path to the road. Go left up the road and take the footpath on the right over the wall, following the wall line SE across the flank of **Sheen Hill**. ▶

After leaving the hill, go over the stile and walk initially E, then SE down through fields to a stile out of view in the hedgerow. Go over the stile and continue down to reach the gate leading across a small stream. Cross the stream and go up the other side, crossing the field to leave via a stile onto a road. Turn left up the road. At the road junction go right, into **Sheen**.

Brund is a tiny community with beautiful honey-coloured buildings. There was once a corn mill here, then a cotton-spinning factory.

If you wish to visit the trig pillar on the hill, access can be gained via a stile further up the road. Permission must be obtained from High Sheen Farm.

The White Peak is still the traditional home for sheep

Sheen church is worth exploring and the gargoyles are spectacular. The lime trees within the grounds of the church are said to have been planted in the 18th century. The house next to the church is known as The Palace. The pub, The Staffordshire Knot, dates back to the time of the Great Fire of London. (The Stafford knot forms part of the insignia of the County of Staffordshire and you will see it on many a waymark sign while out on these walks.)

Walk SW through the village until you reach the Sheen Bunkhouse. Go left and follow the path through the farmyard, descending to a gate. Go through the gate and follow the farm track as it sweeps round to a second gate. Continue through the gate and cross a small field to a wooden gate. ◄

The view of Hartington from this point shows the whole village nestling in the landscape.

Pass through the gate and walk down the hillside to the fenced lane leading to **Bridge-end**, met earlier in the day. Cross the lane and then retrace your steps to return to **Hartington** village.

WALK 32

Hartington to Pilsbury

Start/Finish	Hartington SK 128 604
Distance	9.5 miles (15.5km)
Ascent/Descent	435m
Time	5hr
Terrain	Footpath, trail, fields
Map	OS 1:25000 Explorer OL24
Refreshments	Hartington, Parsley Hay
Parking	Hartington SK 128 604

This is a beautiful walk with fine views out to the NW of the Peak District. The focal point is Pilsbury Castle, but as you walk, the sense of history is ever present and adds to the power of this landscape. The River Dove is always evident, winding its way across pasture; it's pleasing to see it as a small stream without the throngs it attracts in Dovedale.

From the front of the Charles Cotton Hotel in **Hartington** head towards the duck pond then walk W along Stonewell Lane until you reach a new housing development. Turn right through the gate following the Peak and Northern Footpaths sign to Sheen. Follow the path to the left of the power lines through a wooded copse.

Coming out of the trees, go NW using stiles and gates across fields to a small metal bridge and your first encounter with the **River Dove**. Cross the bridge and continue in the same direction to exit the field into a fenced lane leading to **Bridge-end**. Go right, along the lane, then take the footpath left following the sign for Harris Close.

Go up the hillside then follow the tree line along the top of the escarpment, emerging onto open ground. Go left over the stone stile then diagonally right to a gate in the wall. Pass through the gate and follow the wall line NW to **Harris Close**. Take the narrow footpath to the

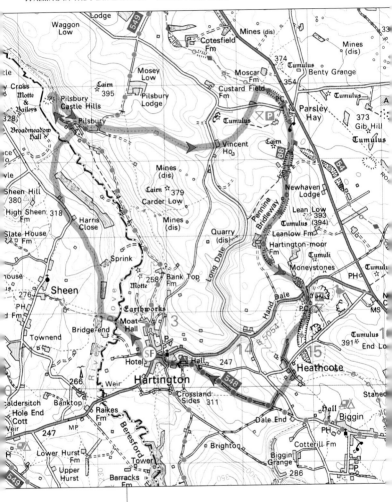

left of the farm buildings, exiting into the farmyard. Turn immediately left, through the squeeze stile and onto the road. Turn right, walking up the road for 450 metres then take the footpath right. Go sharp left through a fenced

Typical White Peak landscape for sheep

garden and proceed through gates to enter a walled and fenced lane running NW. Turn left, walking along the fenced path and exit via a squeeze stile into a field.

Head generally N to the beginning of a line of trees. Go around the head of the tree line, then through a gate continuing N to enter a walled lane. Follow the lane NE to cross a footbridge over the **River Dove**. Follow the track up to the road in **Pilsbury**. Go left, through a gate and follow the road until it turns sharp right. Carry straight on in a NW direction, through the gate and follow the wide bridleway to **Pilsbury Castle**.

The name of **Pilsbury Castle** has roots in Celtic, Saxon and Norman periods, all coming together to name a fortified site. The castle's motte-and-bailey construction dates from the Norman period. These castles were generally built in the years

immediately after the Norman Conquest as fortifications to support military operations and assert control over an area. Wooden buildings, including two baileys, were arranged behind a timber palisade for protection. Access to the castle would be achieved along the sunken track from Pilsbury that is now the bridleway. The situation of the castle would have meant it could protect the crossing of the River Dove at Pilsbury.

From Pilsbury Castle walk SE and take the left-hand track uphill following it E to exit via a gate below a farm building onto a minor road. Go straight across the road, following the sign for Parsley Hay, and take the footpath across field boundaries E to a large pond. Head SE along a wide dry valley to a farm building. Go through the gate and bear left away from the farm building aiming for a waymark post on the horizon.

Follow the path E across fields towards **Vincent House**. Drop down through the gate to the road and cross to enter the farmyard. Follow the footpath through the yard eventually joining a concrete track that takes you onto fields and NE to a minor road by Darley Farm. Follow the footpath through the farm and up the left side of a wall to ascend a small flight of steps onto the **Pennine Bridleway** running along the High Peak Trail.

Go right, along the trail for 100 metres then bear right where the trails split, to follow the Tissington Trail, which

is also the Pennine Bridleway, to Hartington Station – still over a mile (2km) from Hartington. Refreshments can be obtained at Parsley Hay further along the Tissington Trail. The trail was a former railway line, one of the last from the Victorian era to be constructed.

From the signal box at Hartington Station continue along the trail then take the first footpath on the right through a gate and follow the walled lane SW to a stile. Go over this and subsequent stiles following the line of the wall to **Heathcote**.

Enter the village and take the road SE until you come to Chapel Farm. Take the footpath right, through the farm and across the field to a minor road. Cross via the stile and walk up the walled lane directly ahead. At the top turn right into another walled lane and follow this until it meets the road into Hartington. ▶ Turn left, passing Hartington Hall YHA on your right, and walk down to the T-junction. Turn left and return to the centre of **Hartington**.

Hartington Hall YHA is said to have housed Bonnie Prince Charlie during the 18th-century Scottish invasion of England that ended south of Hartington, at Derby.

WALK 33
Hartington to Biggin Dale

Start/Finish	Hartington SK 128 604
Distance	6 miles (10km)
Ascent/Descent	190m
Time	3hr
Terrain	Footpath, trail, fields
Map	OS 1:25000 Explorer OL24
Refreshments	Hartington
Parking	Hartington SK 128 604

Hartington is a wonderful base for exploring the area. Mentioned in the Domesday Book, it takes its name from the Old English words for 'stag' and 'hill'. Stilton cheese is made nearby and sold in the local cheese shop. The Charles Cotton Hotel is named after a local fisherman who made contributions to *The Complete Angler*, written by Izzak Walton and published in the 17th century. The walk follows the River Dove through beautiful dales before returning for a relaxing drink.

The tall spire to your left is sited within the Pike Pool and was a favoured fishing hole for Charles Cotton and Izaak Walton, the author of the classic angling book, The Complete Angler.

From the front of the Charles Cotton Hotel in the centre of **Hartington** walk SW until you reach the public toilets. Follow the steps up the left of the building then turn right after a stile along the footpath that heads S across fields and stiles to enter a wooded area that leads you into **Beresford Dale**. Cross the **River Dove** by the footbridge onto the western bank and continue S, passing the Pike Pool on your left, to a second bridge which returns you to the eastern bank. ◄

Follow the walled track on the left of the field uphill to avoid extremely boggy ground by the river. On reaching a second walled track descending from Crossland Sides running across your direction of travel, turn right and follow the track down to the riverside footpath.

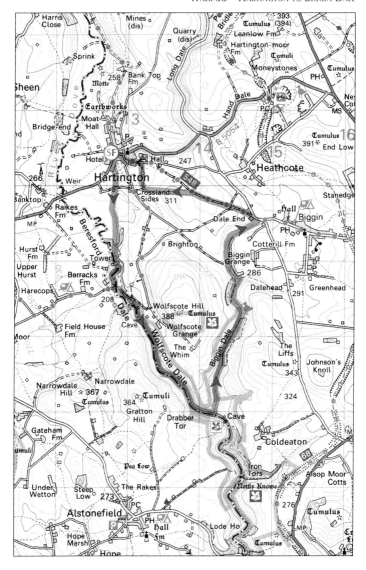

Frank i' th' Rocks, Wolfscote Dale

Enter **Wolfscote Dale** and maintain a south-easterly course for about 1.2 miles (2km) to reach the junction with Biggin Dale.

It is well worth spending time in **Wolfscote Dale**. The limestone cliffs hold caves that can be explored and a wealth of wildflowers in spring and summer. The numerous weirs along the River Dove were constructed to provide a larger feeding area for wild trout and thus improve the fishing. The river sits along a geological boundary between the limestone of the eastern Derbyshire Bank and the shales of Staffordshire, opposite.

Turn NE up **Biggin Dale** and follow the footpath through several gates to reach the road at **Dale End**. Turn left along the road, then take the next lane left, by a house, and follow the walled Highfield Lane. After 1.1km go over the stile on the left and cross fields, W, through several stiles, eventually descending down a short bank into a walled lane. Turn right and walk along the lane to a junction opposite Hartington Hall YHA. Turn left down the road and, at the next junction, go left again to return to the centre of **Hartington** village.

WALK 34

Wetton to Ecton Mine

Start/Finish	Wetton SK 109 551
Distance	6.5 miles (10.5km)
Ascent/Descent	430m
Time	3.5hr
Terrain	Footpath, trail, fields
Map	OS 1:25000 Explorer OL24
Refreshments	Wetton
Parking	Wetton SK 109 551

Wetton, a beautiful 12th-century village, is situated within the lead and copper mining area of the Staffordshire White Peak. This walk leaves the village and crosses the hills and valleys to Ecton Mine, an important copper mine with one of the deepest shafts in England, at 411.5 metres. The return heads down the trail that runs along the Manifold Valley to the foot of Thors Cave, with its 10-metre-high arch.

Turn left out of the car park and then left again at the T-junction to walk through **Wetton** village. After passing the church, go straight ahead where the road turns sharp left, bear right and follow the lane round to the left, following the signs for Back of Ecton. Go through the gate by the reservoir and cross the track to the squeeze stile and gate to follow the footpath towards Wetton Hill. Cross the next stile and follow the wall on the left N downhill. Where the wall turns NW take the right-hand path almost N and exit the open access land after passing a National Trust sign for **Wetton Hill**. Cross the field diagonally right and enter woodland, turning immediately right to reach a minor road.

Go left along the road following it uphill to where it sweeps left, then take the footpath on the right to Broad Ecton Farm. Leave the field by the gate in front of the

Wetton Hill in spring

Do not attempt to enter any of the mine shafts that are in the area.

The Manifold Way follows the line of the former Leek and Manifold Light Railway.

farmhouse, turn left and walk across the farm drive. Follow the wall line directly W to **Top of Ecton**. At the top of the hill go through the gate and head NW to the wall corner then aim for the trees on the skyline, following the signpost for **Ecton Hill**. Go through the gate and follow the path towards the **triangulation pillar**. ◄

From the pillar, head NE to the wall corner and cross the field to the opposite corner, then follow the wall towards the building at Ecton Mine. Go through the gate to observe the information board by the mine shaft. Retrace your steps and follow the wall line SW past the gunpowder store and exit by a house onto a minor road. Turn right, down the hill, then right again at the junction and the next left to cross the bridge and join the Manifold Way on the left. ◄

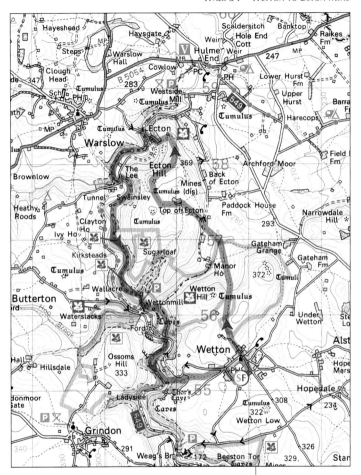

Mining was a major industry in this part of the Peak District, although copper was not as prevalent as other metals, which made the **Ecton copper mine** particularly lucrative. The building housed a Boulton and Watt steam engine that was used to lift ore from the mine workings below ground. The black powder that was used to blast away rock and extend the mine workings was stored in a small building further on in the woodland.

Continue along the Manifold Way. On reaching the road by **Swainsley**, turn left and left again to cross **Ecton Bridge**. As soon as you have crossed, turn right to re-join the Manifold Way on the NE side of the **River Manifold**. Continue along the trail until you reach a gate leading onto a farm track. Go left to the bridge at Wettonmill, but do not cross. ◀

Wetton Mill was once a corn mill, grinding corn from the surrounding fields.

Follow the trail around the right-hand side of the house then take the footpath up a small hill. At the top follow the waymark directions left down then turn right along the trail to a stile leading onto a road. Go straight across the road and the bridge and re-join the Manifold Way following it S until you arrive at a footbridge below **Thor's Cave**. Cross the bridge and follow the footpath up through trees. The access to the cave is on the right, up stone steps.

The River Manifold often disappears in summer down sinkholes that lead into the limestone beds below the surface. **Thor's Cave** was created by the limestone being dissolved by water. The limestone was formed when this area of land was situated over the equator many millions of years ago. Human and animal remains have been found in the cave indicating that it was used as a shelter from the Paleolithic period onwards.

After visiting the cave retrace your steps to the footpath and turn right, going uphill to exit the woodland via a gate into open pasture. Continue up the field in the same direction to exit via a squeeze stile onto a road. Turn right to return to **Wetton**. At the village hall go right to visit the church, then leave the churchyard by the opposite entrance, turning right along the village street to return to the car park.

WALK 35

Alstonefield to Wolfscote Dale

Start/Finish	Alstonefield SK 130 556
Distance	9.5 miles (15km)
Ascent/Descent	470m
Time	5hr
Terrain	Footpath, trail, fields
Map	OS 1:25000 Explorer OL24
Refreshments	Alstonefield, Milldale
Parking	Alstonefield SK 130 556

History shrouds the pre-Norman village of 'Aelstan's open land'. This pretty village was in existence before the Domesday Book. The walk descends to the beautiful Dovedale, entering it by the Pickering Tors. The crystal-clear waters of the River Dove add pleasing background music. The walk, following well-made trails, continues up Wolfscote Dale, with its magnificent limestone tors, before heading back for a welcome pint at The George by the village green in Alstonefield.

From the car park amenity block in Alstonefield, turn right and walk up to the junction then go right, along the road. At the next junction turn left. After 50 metres take the public footpath left, past a house. As it sweeps right go straight ahead into the field following the signpost directions for Stanshope. Follow the right-hand wall to the corner of the field. Go through the gate and continue SW dropping down the hillside to the road by Dale Bottom. Take care in wet weather as the limestone and mud can be slippery.

Go straight across the road and walk up the walled lane almost directly S. Pass by **Grove Farm** and emerge at **Stanshope**. Where the road splits go left, then take the walled lane immediately on your left. After 100 metres go through the gate on the right, following the signpost for

Viator's Bridge, Milldale

Hall Dale. Cross three gates or stiles and enter the dale by the National Trust sign. Walk along the path, gradually losing height until you exit into Dovedale.

Go right, following the sign to Ilam Rock. Cross the bridge at the foot of this limestone pinnacle to reach the wide trail below **Pickering Tor**. Go left, taking the trail to explore the caves at **Dove Holes**, then continue N to reach **Milldale**.

After crossing **Viator's Bridge** at Milldale, go right and right again to follow the road E. ▶

At the next road junction go right, then over the bridge and take the public footpath immediately at the end of the bridge, on the left, to enter the **Wolfscote Dale**. Follow the trail up through Wolfscote Dale for 2.8

Viator's Bridge takes its name from Izaak Walton's work, *The Complete Angler*. In the narrative Walton names himself Viator, meaning traveller.

187

miles (4.5km) until you reach a footbridge just before **Beresford Dale**. Do not cross the bridge but go straight ahead through the gate to cross the ford and follow the footpath across open ground to cross a footbridge leading to a minor road.

Walk down the road then take the National Cycle Route left through the gate and follow it uphill through a second gate. Continue in the same direction until the cycle trail turns sharp right; go straight ahead through a gateway. Ascend **Narrowdale** to the gate at the top then cross farm pasture aiming for the wooded copse on the southern horizon. Follow, on the right, the wall running directly to the foot of the copse. At the top, turn left and go through the gate into the walled lane. Take the footpath on the left out of the lane and follow it to the corner of a small wood. Go through the gate and continue across fields to exit onto a road. Go left and return to **Alstonefield**.

ALSTONEFIELD

On the right of the road is the former village well with steps leading down into the water, while a little further on is the village pump. Looking out from the well onto the western horizon you can see Steep Low. This hill was one of the last sites of execution by gibbet in the country.

Alstonefield is well worth exploring. The church dates from pre-Norman times and has a Norman arch in the chancel. In the area of the village green you'll find the pub, the former general store and post office and the three-storey workhouse. The village was a major transport hub for the lead mining industry, and several holloways used by the packhorse trains can be seen radiating from the centre. Much of the surrounding land was enclosed around the 1840s. Until fairly recently, the hills were covered with ash trees, but they were cut down to provide fuel for lead smelting.

WALK 36
Froghall to Cheddleton

Start/Finish	Froghall Wharf SK 026 476
Distance	11 miles (17.5km)
Ascent/Descent	340m
Time	5hr
Terrain	Footpath, trail, fields
Map	OS 1:25000 Explorer OL24, and Derby 259
Refreshments	Froghall Wharf, Cheddleton Station, Consall Station
Parking	Froghall Wharf SK 026 476

This walk offers something of a rare experience in the White Peak, the chance to walk alongside a beautiful canal and a steam railway, with great country pubs and cafés along the way. There is also some wonderful scenery to be enjoyed but that might just be overloading the senses. Keep your eyes peeled as you pass through the woodlands for barn owls, buzzards and kingfishers.

> The canal setting with the wonderful café and park land at **Froghall Wharf** would belie the industrial past of the area were it not for the huge limekilns situated there. Limestone brought by canal and rail from the quarries was burnt here to provide quick-lime and cement products. The area was also home to a large copper processing factory that produced the very first transatlantic cable.

From the car park and visitor centre at **Froghall**, walk up the steps to the left of the limekiln on the SE side of the car park. Turn left at the top and follow the track past the cottages until you reach a fork. Take the signposted left-hand footpath up the holloway until you arrive at wooden steps on the left. Descend the steps into Harston Wood Nature Reserve and follow the footpath through

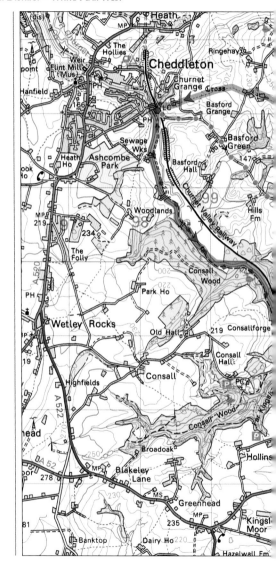

the woodland to exit via a stile into open ground. Shortly after, follow the directions of the short waymarker on the right, almost hidden in the hedgerow, turning left here to take the footpath up a steep hillside to a gate and stile. Continue straight ahead along the farm track until you reach the road. Go right and take the next footpath on the right, bearing left at the two junctions until you arrive at the road into **Foxt**. Walk up into the village taking the next road left to the pub.

Continue past the pub and take the footpath on the left, opposite the bus stop. Follow the footpath NW across fields and stiles to reach a minor road at **Cloughhead**. Walk NW down the road until the footpath forks off to the left just in front of a house. Continue down the footpath into woodland descending through the trees to cross a stream and ascend to a road opposite. Walk along this minor road until you enter the village of **Ipstones**.

Follow the road around to the left, bearing right at the next junction. Walk through the village until you come to a footpath on the left just as the road sweeps right. Follow the footpath W to the **B5053**. Cross the road and turn right, then take the footpath on the left, between houses, W across fields. Exit into a lane just W of farm buildings. Walk left along the lane then continue along the footpath at the edge of fields to a wall corner. Go through the stile and bear diagonally right across the field, then through a squeeze stile. Walk straight ahead to leave the field by a second squeeze stile at the left of the gate. Follow the road right, through the delightfully named **Noonsun Common**, and at the next junction go left, then immediately right along the public footpath. Continue NE past the farm, exiting via the track onto a minor road. Walk right, to arrive at Stocks Green. ◄

Continue past the church and turn left at the next junction then take the left-hand track. Shortly after, bear left at the bend across the grass to a squeeze stile. Cross the field diagonally right, aiming for the left side of a cottage seen in trees on the horizon. Exit the field via a squeeze stile onto a road and go straight ahead through a farm gate by a barn. Follow the track down until it

The Church of St Leonard is worth visiting to view the wonderful rood screen.

sweeps right. Then take the stile on the left and follow the left wall to cross a stile into a narrow, walled lane. On reaching a minor road go straight across following the public footpath across a field onto a private drive by **Whitehough Hall**.

Walk across the front of the house, through the gap in the wall and bear right by the stone gazebo to a squeeze stile. Squeeze through and turn left, maintaining a NW direction as the path passes over small hills and valleys. Keep to the right of a small barn to reach a stile leading into woodland. Go over the stile and follow the way-markers left through two gates to enter the RSPB Reserve. Follow the public footpath through the reserve over a very narrow bridge across **Coombes Brook**. Ascend the opposite side to go through a gate leading into a field. Take the footpath through the squeeze stile, aiming to keep to the right of the farm buildings on the horizon. Cross a lane then at the road go left, then right at the next footpath. Follow the path generally W to the stone cross in the corner of a field.

The medieval Butter Cross above Cheddleton

This is the Cheddleton or **Challinor Butter Cross**. It marks the crossing of two ancient routes across the land. There are several examples of this type of cross in the surrounding areas and they are thought to have been located where goods – butter being one – were stacked upon the stone steps to be sold. It seems improbable now; its location being so remote from any community, but this is a good example of how time can erase the purpose of many things in the landscape.

Ignore the stile to the left of the cross. Continue straight on from the cross maintaining a westerly

Park House Wood Lift Bridge on the Caldon Canal

direction. Go over the stile to the next field and follow the hedgerow down to the road. Cross to the footpath opposite and skirt the farmyard, crossing the farm track, then heads on down towards **Cheddleton Station**. Bear right near the bottom of the field and go through the gate then turn left along the track to the road. Walk down Basford Bridge Lane and cross the stone bridge, then go left onto the canal towpath and follow it SE.

The **Caldon Canal** was built at the very end of the 18th century to transport limestone to the Midlands. It became obsolete after the railway was built alongside it in the mid 19th century. Today canal boats ply the route between Froghall Wharf and Etruria on the Trent and Mersey Canal. Rail passenger services ceased in 1965 and the line closed in 1988, but volunteers have redeveloped it, running both steam and diesel trains. The canal has many interesting features, including a variety of bridges and locks. At Consall Station, there is a superb pub overlooking the canal and railway.

Continue SE along the canal-side trail. On reaching the **B5053** at **Froghall**, cross the road and follow the footpath back to the car park at Froghall Wharf.

WALK 37

Waterhouses to Grindon

Start/Finish	Waterhouses SK 085 501
Distance	8.5 miles (13.5km)
Ascent/Descent	275m
Time	4hr
Terrain	Footpath, trail, fields
Map	OS 1:25000 Explorer OL24
Refreshments	Waterhouses
Parking	Waterhouses SK 085 501

Waterhouses sits on the boundary of the Peak District National Park, marking its most south-westerly point. The walk takes you across the pleasing and gentle farmland of the White Peak to the village of Grindon, with its interesting stone carvings. The return is via the Manifold Way, along the disued Leek and Manifold Light Railway route, to Waterhouses. This is a nice gentle amble with wonderful views.

Walk out of the Peak District National Park car park at **Waterhouses** via the vehicle exit and turn right down to the **A523**. Cross the road and go left until you have passed the War Memorial on your left and the road begins to sweep left. Then take the signposted public footpath towards a residential double garage. Just before the driveway forks, go through the gate in the left-hand wall and follow the right-hand boundary of a small enclosure to exit via a gate. Carry straight ahead through the gate opposite and then follow the footpath through two more gates to emerge onto a sports recreation field. Go right and take the footpath around the boundary to the NE corner and ascend a short bank to cross over a stile into a field. Follow the footpath generally N across several fields, using stiles and gates, to a lane. Continue through a gate and past farm buildings on your left to a

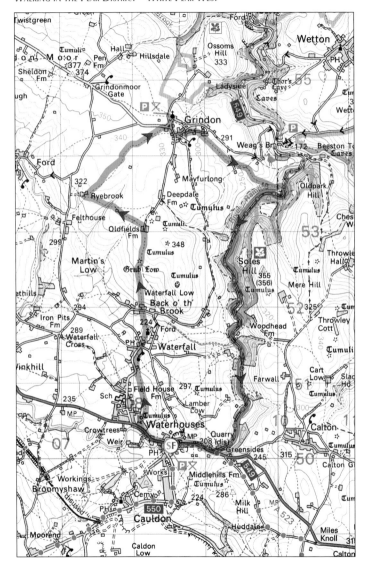

The picturesque village of Waterfall

stile giving access to a large field. Bear diagonally right aiming for a red-roofed cottage. Exit the field via a gate to enter the village of **Waterfall**.

> **Waterfall** is a pretty little place with its village pump and stocks sitting on the tiny green. The church of St James and St Bartholomew, hidden away behind trees, dates from the 12th century and has an impressive chancel arch from that period.

Head NE past the village green and follow the road to the right of the house. Then take the footpath through the squeeze stile into a field and follow the right-hand boundary until you reach a gate on the right leading to the church. Exit the churchyard via the gate in its northern boundary and bear left across the field, passing through a gate, then cross a footbridge over a brook to exit onto a minor road at **Back o' th' Brook**. Go left a few metres and take the footpath N through the gate up to farm buildings and straight ahead along the left boundary.

After crossing a stile, continue along the boundary until it starts to veer NW and go diagonally right, across the field to a gate in the NE corner. Go through the gate and follow the wall to the lane taking you through **Oldfields Farm**. Just after the farm buildings take the footpath on the left across fields to a small ravine. Cross the brook by the concrete water tank and go over the stone stile in the wall then ascend the slope following the faint boundary line, use the trees as a guide, to a squeeze stile leading to **Ryebrook**.

On reaching the fence around the farm go right and follow the footpath NE for 1 mile (1.5km) through several stiles and gates to emerge via a stone stile over a wall onto the minor road to **Grindon**. Turn right then bear left at the next junction to arrive at the church to admire the stone carvings. ◄

Walk back to the junction and go left, following the road past the village pinfold (the Anglo-Saxon term for an animal enclosure) and then the village hall. Just before the road sweeps right take the footpath on the right, across the front of a cottage and enter a narrow lane. Do not go through the gate ahead of you but turn left and follow the walled lane behind houses until you reach a gate on the right. Walk SE across fields through several gates

Find the dragon, dog, monkey and snake, as well as the man poking his tongue out, the one grinning and the one laughing.

The monkey chasing the snake on Grindon church tower

and stiles to a disused dewpond. Go to the right of the structure and through the gate to descend along a wide grassy track to the Manifold Way by the **River Hamps**. Turn right along the tarmac trail crossing the river over several bridges for 2.7 miles (4.4km) until you reach the **A523**. Cross the road and go right until you come to the entrance to the **Waterhouses** car park on the left and the end of the walk.

The bed of the Rive Hamps. The water has gone underground at the Swallett Hole near Waterhouses

RIVER HAMPS

In summer it seems a strange thing to call the rock-strewn thread that runs beside the bed of the Leek and Manifold Light Railway a 'river'. There is no water. This unusual state is due to the limestone geology of the White Peak. The River Hamps that you should be walking alongside begins high above the valley near Feltysitch, south-east of Upper Hulme. It then travels south to Waterhouses, where it turns north to join the River Manifold below Beeston Tor. The name 'Hamps' derives from 'Hafhesp, Hamhesp' meaning 'dry in summer'. During summer months the river disappears underground at Cotton Swallet, near Waterhouses, and re-emerges at Hamps Springs in Ilam Park.

WALK 38
Ilam to Dovedale

Start/Finish	Ilam SK 131 506
Distance	7 miles (11km)
Ascent/Descent	370m
Time	3.5hr
Terrain	Footpath, trail, fields
Map	OS 1:25000 Explorer OL24
Refreshments	Ilam Hall
Parking	Ilam SK 131 506

Many say Dovedale is the most beautiful dale and it certainly has a very good claim to be. The walk starts at Ilam Hall and rises above the Manifold Valley to Casterne Hall, featured in many period dramas on TV and film. From there you descend via Hall Dale into the idyllic Dovedale and follow a wide trail, visiting along the way Reynards Cave, Ilam Rock, Tissington Spires and Lover's Leap, before returning to Ilam Hall.

The remains of the 11th-century 'Battle Stone' is said to have possible connections with fighting between Saxons and Danes.

Take the steps down from the National Trust teashop at **Ilam Hall** to the riverside walk and turn right following the path past the remains of a stone cross protected by railings, then through successive gates until you reach a minor road by River Lodge. ◄

Turn left and follow the road bearing left where it forks then take the footpath on the right just before **Rushley Bridge** spanning the **River Manifold**. Follow the footpath virtually N, going through a hedgerow and past a lovely old barn on your right before a short ascent via two gates to a farm track.

Go left and take the footpath immediately on the right up a slope and through a gate to follow a wall line to re-join the track in front of **Castern Hall**.

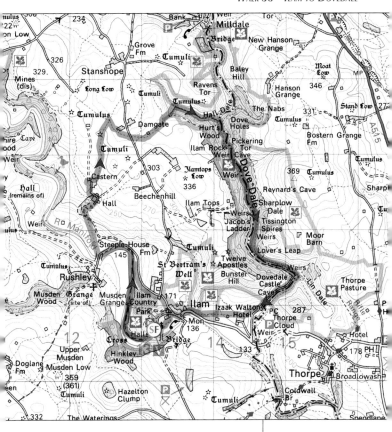

As with much of the surrounding land, the monks of Burton Abbey were the original owners of **Castern Hall**. In the 16th century, after the Dissolution of the Monasteries, the house passed to the Hurt family, who still resides there today. The house was remodelled in the 18th century in the Georgian style. It has featured in several TV and film productions, including; *Jane Eyre*, *Far from the Madding Crowd* and *Peaky Blinders*.

Castern Hall

Sheep shearing is a frenzy of activity that takes place every summer in the White Peak.

Follow the track around the house, keeping left where it splits until you reach a footpath on the right just before **Castern**. Go through the gate and ascend the hillside and through the gate at the top. Go right, noting the view of Beeston Tor to your left, and exit the field via a gate to cross a concrete track to the farm. Go through the gate opposite and follow the footpath along the boundary fence of the farm then turn N to a stone stile in a wall. Cross the stile to follow the fingerpost N keeping the wall to your left. Go through four boundary gates until a wall ahead blocks the way. Ignore the stone stile in the wall and follow the fingerpost SE to **Damgate**. ◀

Keep to the right of the farm and pass through the gate then immediately go left through a second gate and cross the field diagonally right to exit via another gate onto a minor road. Go right then take the footpath next left down a walled lane to a derelict barn. Keep to the right of the building to go through a gate and continue down a walled lane, passing a dewpond on the left. At the end of the lane go left.

The **limekiln** on the right is one of many hundreds that you will come across in the White Peak. Beside

it is the small quarry used to provide stone for the lime burning. The burnt lime was used to make cement for buildings and also to treat the fields to improve the pasture for the sheep.

Go through the gate and enter the National Trust Allen's Bank. Go left downhill following the wall line and cross a stile in **Hurt's Wood**. Follow the path down through the trees until the landscape opens out and a stile gives access to **Hall Dale**. Go right through the gate and follow the dale down to the **River Dove**.

Turn right through the gap in the wall to walk down **Dovedale** keeping to the W bank of the river until you reach **Ilam Rock**, a prominent limestone spire. Cross the bridge to reach the eastern bank and follow this S. As you progress take note of the various limestone formations that peek through the heavily wooded slopes. **Pickering Tor** is immediately visible as you step off the bridge. After crossing the boardwalk, **Reynard's Cave**, located behind a natural stone arch, is accessible up a steep rocky slope to your left. Further on are the limestone **Tissington Spires** and, further on again, the limestone steps take you up to **Lover's Leap** and the **The Twelve Apostles** limestone pinnacles.

LOVER'S LEAP

There are so many stories connected with Lover's Leap, stretching from the Middle Ages through the Napoleonic Wars to the Second World War, but none of them are verifiable. They all centre on a young woman who either believed that her lover had been killed, or who was prevented from marrying him due to his higher status. As she jumped off the promontory, the trees saved her either by holding her in the branches or by catching her bloomers as she fell. Perhaps the most interesting aspect of Lover's Leap is to be found in the steps. Look down and you will see strange screw-like shapes. These are the fossilised remains of crinoids, sea creatures that were abundant millions of years ago when a tropical ocean covered Dovedale. Their appearance gave rise to them being known locally as 'Derbyshire screws'.

The stepping stones across the River Dove

Continue down the steps and along the trail until you reach the famous stepping stones crossing the River Dove at the foot of **Lin Dale**. Go across the stones and turn left along the drive to reach the National Trust car park. Go right, out of the car park, and cross the lane to ascend steps through trees then through a gate onto pasture. Follow the footpath across the fields W passing the **Izaak Walton Hotel** on your left. Cross through several gate and stile combinations until the path leads you onto a minor road. Go right, along the road to return to **Ilam Hall**.

WALK 39

Ilam to Beeston Tor

Start/Finish	Ilam SK 131 506
Distance	10 miles (16km)
Ascent/Descent	510m
Time	5hr
Terrain	Footpath, fields
Map	OS 1:25000 Explorer OL24
Refreshments	Ilam Hall
Parking	Ilam SK 131 506

This walk across the rolling landscape of the White Peak is gentle and takes in several points of interest along the way. Lovers of geology will enjoy Beeston Tor, a looming cliff that sits above the disappearing River Manifold that rises again by Ilam Hall. The remains of Throwley Hall, a surprise in its exposed position, remind us that history is ever present in the area.

The large **stone cross** positioned at the junction near the bridge at Ilam is modelled on an Eleanor Cross. It was designed by George Gilbert Scott who worked on much of the transformation of Ilam for his friend Jesse Watts Russell, the owner of the Ilam Estate. The cross was erected as a memorial to his wife, Mary, and is made of local sandstone around the base, Cotswold stone for the central structure and Caen limestone for the statutes.

From the large cross in Ilam, walk NE along the road bearing right by the entrance to the hall grounds. Take the footpath next left over the stile and follow it across the grounds, initially SW, then veering diagonally right across a ridge-and-furrow field system, then dropping down to a distinct path. Turn right, then go left, across the footbridge over the **River Manifold** and bear right, across fields to

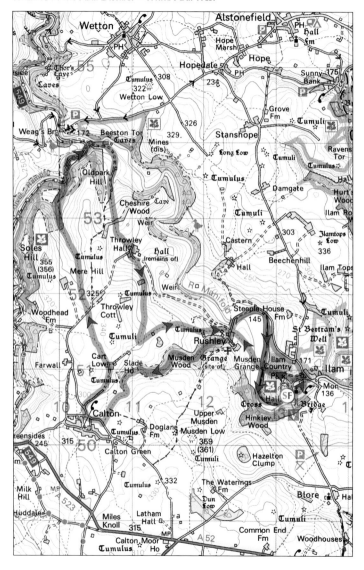

The Ilam Cross modelled on an Eleanor Cross

Musden Grange. At the road go left to **Rushley** then, just after the cattle grid in the road, take the footpath left, through the gates to cross a field and enter **Musden Wood** via a stile. ▸

Continue through the narrow, wooded valley, crossing three fences by gates or stiles and emerging into open fields. Follow the left-hand hedge SW across fields, then onto the road leading into **Calton**. Turn right, along the road and right again at the next junction. Take the first footpath on the right, following the narrow lane through a stile and three gates to arrive at **Slade House**. Follow the track NW across successive cattle grids until you reach a minor road. Go straight across, keeping to the left of a large round stone structure, to enter a wide valley by a gate. Follow the wall on your left through a second

In spring and early summer this wood is full of the heady aroma of wild garlic, *Allium ursinum*.

gate then keep right where the path splits and enter Old Soles Wood through a gate. Follow the rocky and slippery footpath down to emerge onto the Manifold Way. Go right along the tarmac track until you reach **Weag's Barn Nature Reserve** on the left, then take the footpath just after on the right across a field to **Beeston Tor** standing guard above the confluence of the River Manifold and River Hamps.

After crossing the bridge over the **River Hamps** to reach Beeston Tor Farm take the right fork uphill towards Throwley Hall. Follow the track through two gates, passing a wonderful barn on the left as you go. After the last gate, walk up the hillside aiming for the left of a large copse that is situated to your right on the skyline. At the copse follow the wall line through a gate and head generally SE across a field to exit into the farmyard at Throwley Hall. Bear right and then left through the farm and follow the road SE to the remains of the old **Throwley Hall**.

The remains of Throwley Hall

The ruins of **Throwley Hall** stand high above the Manifold Valley. The village of Throwley also existed on the site until the early 16th century. Looking at the farmhouse and ruins today you can detect the remains of the deer park in the outline of the fields and boundaries of drystone walls that surrounded the hall. The hall was abandoned in the late 19th century and, with falling land prices and new taxation of the

*Beeston Tor
from Castern*

landed gentry, the roof was removed in the 1920s and the hall fell into disrepair.

After passing the old hall, take the footpath on the right across fields until you reach a narrow, walled lane running SW. Go left and follow the wall to a gate, then go diagonally right, across a field. Follow the wall SE until you reach a gate just before the ruin of a barn. Go through the gate and down the hill passing through two more gates until you exit onto the road at **Rushley**. Go left following the road down over the stone bridge and keeping to the right where it intersects the track to Castern Hall. After passing over a cattle grid by River Lodge, take the footpath on the right, through the gates and join the track S to **Ilam Country Park**. Keep by the riverside path until just after a stone pillar on the left known locally as the 'Battle Stone'. ▶

The 'Battle Stone' marks the battles between the Saxons and the Danes for control of the surrounding land.

Where the path splits take the left fork uphill to emerge in front of the National Trust café overlooking **Ilam Hall** and gardens. From the hall follow the driveway to the road and the end of the walk.

WALK 40
Ilam to Blore

Start/Finish	Ilam SK 131 506
Distance	5.5 miles (9km)
Ascent/Descent	275m
Time	3hr
Terrain	Footpath, fields
Map	OS 1:25000 Explorer OL24
Refreshments	Ilam Hall
Parking	Ilam SK 131 506

The village of Ilam may seem out of place in the Peak District to the new visitor. Swiss chalet-style houses sit by a 19th-century mansion and park. The National Trust now owns this vision of Jesse Watts Russell, while the remains of the neo-Gothic Ilam Hall is an impressive YHA hostel. This lovely walk across rolling countryside takes in one of the most beautiful churches in the area.

From Ilam Hall walk through the park to the entrance at the main road and turn right to the large memorial cross in the centre of **Ilam**. Walk SE across the bridge and take the left-hand footpath down to the **River Manifold**. Proceed downstream along the footpath crossing several stiles and fields. After passing through a gate at the end of the narrow woods, walk straight on until you meet the track running down to **Coldwall Bridge**.

Go right following the track uphill and through a farm gate to **Coldwall Farm**. Go through the farm following the driveway as it winds right then, at the road, go straight across and through a squeeze stile into a field. Follow the footpath SW downhill and at the bottom turn right, following the narrowing valley sides to a road. Go over the stile in the corner of the field and turn right along the road to **Blore** and enter the churchyard.

The Norman church of **St Bartholomew** is one of the loveliest in these parts. Built at the turn of the 12th century it contains many additions from Norman, Tudor and Jacobean periods. Inside is the alabaster Bassett tomb. The Bassett family lived at Blore Hall, opposite the church, and are ancestors

Ilam Hall

of the present-day Queen. The church suffered during the Reformation and evidence of this can be seen in the sawn stumps behind the rood screen.

Walk towards the S gate of the churchyard but do not go through. Go right, to the top SW corner, and pass through the narrow squeeze stile into a private garden. Follow the public footpath SW to cross a stile into a field. Follow the right-hand wall and drop down into the valley bottom via the grass track then go over the wall stile just after the end of woodland. Continue along the valley bottom until you reach a stile leading onto a road. Go left along the road and take the next footpath on the right. Follow the path NW across two fields and, after the second wall, go W uphill to a gate. Go through the gate and follow the wall right, noting the Ordnance Survey **triangulation pillar** site on your left. Continue along the path as it turns NE through two large stone gateposts. ◀

Pass the ruins of **Upper Musden** on your left until you come to a farm track. Turn left towards the ruins until you come to a gate. Go through the gate and turn immediately

There is an excellent view of Thorpe Cloud and the entrance to Dovedale from this point.

right, going over a stone stile in the wall corner then turning right again over another wall to enter a field. Head diagonally left across the field to a stone stile. ▶

Cross the wall and walk N passing through a gate to start a descent towards **Musden Grange** along a well-defined grass track. As the track sweeps right, follow the footpath down the steep hillside E, crossing two walls to the gate leading to the footbridge across the **River Manifold**.

Cross the bridge and turn right along the wide trail, keeping right where it forks. Just after St Bertram's Well, ascend the stone steps leading to **Ilam Hall**. From the hall go right, through the churchyard.

In the churchyard are two Saxon stone cross shafts. Inside the **Church of the Holy Cross**, the Norman font is carved with humans and dragons, while in the south chapel is the shrine and remains of St Bertram. In the north chapel is the tomb of Jesse Watts Russell.

In spring this meadow is full of wildflowers, a beautiful sight against a blue sky.

Meadow flowers in the White Peak

APPENDIX A
Route summary table

Walk	Start/Finish		Distance	Time	Page
Northern section					
1	Castleton to Mam Tor	Castleton SK 147 829	4.5 miles (7.5km)	3hr	31
2	Winnats Pass to Cave Dale	Castleton SK 149 829	7.5 miles (12km)	3.5hr	35
3	Windgather Rocks	Errwood Reservoir SK 013 756	6.5 miles (10.5km)	3.5hr	41
4	Goyt Valley	Whaley Bridge SK 008 798	12.5 miles (20km)	6hr	45
5	Bollington to Swanscoe	Bollington SJ 930 780	7 miles (11km)	3.5hr	51
6	Lamaload to Shining Tor	Lamaload Reservoir SJ 975 753	8 miles (13km)	4.5hr	55
7	Tideswell to Hay Dale	Tideswell SK 152 757	7 miles (11km)	3.5hr	60
8	Buxton	Buxton SK 058 735	3.5 miles (6km)	2hr	64
9	Buxton to Castle Naze	Buxton SK 057 744	8.5 miles (13.5km)	4hr	68
10	Burbage to the Goyt Valley	Burbage SK 035 723	6 miles (10km)	3.5hr	72
11	Millers Dale to Wormhill	Millers Dale SK 138 732	7 miles (11km)	3.5hr	76
12	Millers Dale to Deep Dale	Millers Dale SK 138 732	11 miles (18km)	6hr	80
13	Trentabank to Sutton Common	Trentabank SJ 961 711	9.5 miles (15km)	4.5hr	87
14	Tegg's Nose to Macclesfield Forest	Tegg's Nose SJ 950 732	8 miles (13km)	4.5hr	92
15	Shutlingsloe to Chest Hollow	Clough House Farm SJ 987 698	6.5 miles (10.5km)	4hr	97

Walk	Start/Finish		Distance	Time	Page
16	Three Shires Head	Gradbach Mill SJ 993 660	6 miles (9.5km)	3hr	101
17	Rushton Spencer to Danebridge	Rushton Spencer SJ 940 623	8 miles (12.5km)	4hr	105
18	Lud's Church	Gradbach Mill SJ 993 660	5.5 miles (9km)	3hr	110
19	The Dragon's Back	Earl Sterndale SK 089 670	4.5 miles (7.5km)	3hr	114
20	Flash to Axe Edge	Flash SK 025 671	7.5 miles (12km)	4hr	118
Southern section					
21	The Roaches	The Roaches SK 003 621	5.5 miles (9km)	3hr	125
22	Hollinsclough to Hollins Hill	Hollinsclough SK 065 665	3.5 miles (6km)	2hr	131
23	Longnor to High Wheeldon	Longnor SK 088 649	4.5 miles (7km)	2.5hr	135
24	Hen Cloud	Upper Hulme SK 013 609	4.5 miles (7.5km)	2.5hr	138
25	Upper Hulme to Blake Mere	Upper Hulme SK 013 609	5.5 miles (8.5km)	3hr	142
26	Upper Elkstone to Lumbs Farm	Upper Elkstone SK 055 590	6 miles (9.5km)	3hr	146
27	Leek to Gun	Leek SJ 984 565	14.5 miles (23.5km)	7hr	150
28	Onecote to Old Mixon Hay	Onecote SK 049 551	6 miles (9.5km)	3hr	157
29	Hulme End to Revidge	Hulme End SK 103 593	6 miles (9.5km)	3hr	161
30	Grindon to Butterton	Grindon SK 084 545	7 miles (11km)	3.5hr	165
31	Hartington to Sheen	Hartington SK 128 604	7 miles (11km)	3hr	169
32	Hartington to Pilsbury	Hartington SK 128 604	9.5 miles (15.5km)	5hr	173
33	Hartington to Biggin Dale	Hartington SK 128 604	6 miles (10km)	3hr	178

Walk	Start/Finish		Distance	Time	Page
34	Wetton to Ecton Mine	Wetton SK 109 551	6.5 miles (10.5km)	3.5hr	181
35	Alstonefield to Wolfscote Dale	Alstonefield SK 130 556	9.5 miles (15km)	5hr	185
36	Froghall to Cheddleton	Froghall Wharf SK 026 476	11 miles (17.5km)	5hr	189
37	Waterhouses to Grindon	Waterhouses SK 085 501	8.5 miles (13.5km)	4hr	195
38	Ilam to Dovedale	Ilam SK 131 506	7 miles (11km)	3.5hr	200
39	Ilam to Beeston Tor	Ilam SK 131 506	10 miles (16km)	5hr	205
40	Ilam to Blore	Ilam SK 131 506	5.5 miles (9km)	3hr	210

APPENDIX B
Useful websites

Accommodation
www.visitpeakdistrict.com/
accommodation

British Mountaineering Council
www.thebmc.co.uk

Mountain Rescue Search Dogs England
www.mountainrescuesearchdogs
england.org.uk

Open Access
www.openaccess.naturalengland.org.uk

Peak and Northern Footpaths Society
www.pnfs.org.uk

Peak District National Park
www.peakdistrict.gov.uk

Royal Society for the Protection of Birds
www.rspb.org.uk

The Ramblers
www.ramblers.org.uk

The Random Apple Company
www.swanscoe.co.uk

The Wildlife Trusts
www.wildlifetrusts.org

Transport
www.peakdistrict.gov.uk/visiting/
publictransport

YHA
www.yha.org.uk

Peak District Mountain Rescue Teams
For emergency callout always dial
999 and ask for Police, then Mountain
Rescue

Buxton Mountain Rescue
www.buxtonmountainrescue.org.uk

Derby Mountain Rescue
www.derbymrt.org.uk

Edale Mountain Rescu
www.edalemrt.co.uk

Glossop Mountain Rescue
www.gmrt.org.uk

Kinder Mountain Rescue
www.kmrt.org.uk

Oldham Mountain Rescue
www.omrt.org

Woodhead Mountain Rescue
www.woodheadmrt.org

APPENDIX C
Bibliography and further reading

Besley, P (2017). *Dark Peak Walks*. Kendal, Cicerone Press.

Besley, P (2020). *Walking in the Peak District – White Peak East*. Kendal, Cicerone Press.

Boatman, D (1982). *The natural history of Britain and Northern Europe. Fields and Lowlands*. London, Hodder and Stoughton Limited.

Edwards, KC, Swinnerton, HH, Hall, RH (1973). *The Peak District*. Glasgow, Collins.

Evans, P (2018). *How to see nature*. London, Batsford.

Hurst, I, Bennett, R (2007). *Mountain Rescue. History and Development in the Peak District 1920s–Present Day*. Stroud, The History Press.

Pevsner, N (1953). *The buildings of England. Derbyshire*. London, Penguin Books Limited.

Wood, E (2007). *The South-West Peak: History of the Landscape*. Ashbourne, Landmark Publishing Limited.

DOWNLOAD THE ROUTES
IN GPX FORMAT

All the routes in this guide are available for download from:

www.cicerone.co.uk/977/GPX

as GPX files. You should be able to load them into most formats of mobile device, whether GPS or smartphone.

When you go to this link, you will be asked for your email address and where you purchased the guide, and have the option to subscribe to the Cicerone e-newsletter.

www.cicerone.co.uk

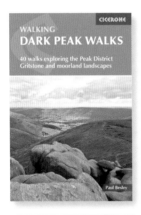
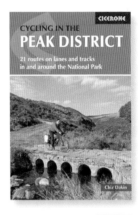
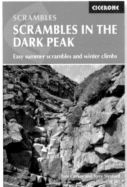
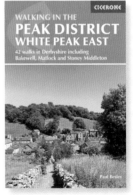

LISTING OF CICERONE GUIDES

BRITISH ISLES CHALLENGES, COLLECTIONS AND ACTIVITIES

Cycling Land's End to John o' Groats
The Big Rounds
The Book of the Bothy
The C2C Cycle Route
The End to End Cycle Route
The Mountains of England and Wales: Vol 1 Wales
The Mountains of England and Wales: Vol 2 England
The National Trails
Walking The End to End Trail

SCOTLAND

Backpacker's Britain: Northern Scotland
Ben Nevis and Glen Coe
Cycle Touring in Northern Scotland
Cycling in the Hebrides
Great Mountain Days in Scotland
Mountain Biking in Southern and Central Scotland
Mountain Biking in West and North West Scotland
Not the West Highland Way Scotland
Scotland's Best Small Mountains
Scotland's Mountain Ridges
Skye's Cuillin Ridge Traverse
The Ayrshire and Arran Coastal Paths
The Borders Abbeys Way
The Great Glen Way
The Great Glen Way Map Booklet
The Hebridean Way
The Hebrides
The Isle of Mull
The Isle of Skye
The Skye Trail
The Southern Upland Way
The Speyside Way
The Speyside Way Map Booklet
The West Highland Way
The West Highland Way Map Booklet
Walking Highland Perthshire
Walking in the Cairngorms
Walking in the Pentland Hills
Walking in the Scottish Borders
Walking in the Southern Uplands
Walking in Torridon
Walking Loch Lomond and the Trossachs
Walking on Arran
Walking on Harris and Lewis
Walking on Jura, Islay and Colonsay
Walking on Rum and the Small Isles
Walking on the Orkney and Shetland Isles

Walking on Uist and Barra
Walking the Cape Wrath Trail
Walking the Corbetts
    Vol 1 South of the Great Glen
    Vol 2 North of the Great Glen
Walking the Galloway Hills
Walking the Munros
    Vol 1 – Southern, Central and Western Highlands
    Vol 2 – Northern Highlands and the Cairngorms
Winter Climbs Ben Nevis and Glen Coe
Winter Climbs in the Cairngorms

NORTHERN ENGLAND TRAILS

Hadrian's Wall Path
Hadrian's Wall Path Map Booklet
The Coast to Coast Walk
The Coast to Coast Walk Map Booklet
The Dales Way
The Dales Way Map Booklet
The Pennine Way
The Pennine Way Map Booklet
Walking the Tour of the Lake District

NORTH EAST ENGLAND, YORKSHIRE DALES AND PENNINES

Cycling in the Yorkshire Dales
Great Mountain Days in the Pennines
Mountain Biking in the Yorkshire Dales
St Oswald's Way and St Cuthbert's Way
The Cleveland Way and the Yorkshire Wolds Way
The Cleveland Way Map Booklet
The North York Moors
The Reivers Way
The Teesdale Way
Trail and Fell Running in the Yorkshire Dales
Walking in County Durham
Walking in Northumberland
Walking in the North Pennines
Walking in the Yorkshire Dales: North and East
Walking in the Yorkshire Dales: South and West

NORTH WEST ENGLAND THE ISLE OF MAN

Cycling the Pennine Bridleway
Cycling the Way of the Roses
Hadrian's Cycleway
Isle of Man Coastal Path

The Lancashire Cycleway
The Lune Valley and Howgills
Walking in Cumbria's Eden Valley
Walking in Lancashire
Walking in the Forest of Bowland and Pendle
Walking on the Isle of Man
Walking on the West Pennine Moors
Walks in Silverdale and Arnside

LAKE DISTRICT

Cycling in the Lake District
Great Mountain Days in the Lake District
Lake District Winter Climbs
Lake District: High Level and Fell Walks
Lake District: Low Level and Lake Walks
Mountain Biking in the Lake District
Outdoor Adventures with Children – Lake District
Scrambles in the Lake District – North
Scrambles in the Lake District – South
The Cumbria Way
Trail and Fell Running in the Lake District
Walking the Lake District Fells:
    Borrowdale
    Buttermere
    Coniston
    Keswick
    Langdale
    Mardale and the Far East
    Patterdale
    Wasdale

DERBYSHIRE, PEAK DISTRICT AND MIDLANDS

Cycling in the Peak District
Dark Peak Walks
Scrambles in the Dark Peak
Walking in Derbyshire
Walking in the Peak District – White Peak East

SOUTHERN ENGLAND

20 Classic Sportive Rides in South East England
20 Classic Sportive Rides in South West England
Cycling in the Cotswolds
Mountain Biking on the North Downs
Mountain Biking on the South Downs
Suffolk Coast and Heath Walks
The Cotswold Way
The Cotswold Way Map Booklet

For full information on all our guides,
books and eBooks, visit our website:
www.cicerone.co.uk